Writing a Research Paper

Writing a Research Paper

Revised Edition

Lionel Menasche

 Pitt Series in English as a Second Language

Ann Arbor

THE UNIVERSITY OF MICHIGAN PRESS

For Felicity, Renee, and Edward

Revised edition © by the University of Michigan 1997
First published by the University of Michigan Press 1993
First edition copyright © 1984, University of Pittsburgh Press and the English
    Language Institute, University of Pittsburgh
All rights reserved
ISBN 0-472-08369-4
Library of Congress Catalog Card No. 83-12492
Published in the United States of America by
The University of Michigan Press
Manufactured in the United States of America

2001   2000   1999   1998   5   4   3   2

Preface to the Revised Edition

AUDIENCE AND PURPOSE

This textbook has been designed to help advanced English as a second language (ESL) students become accustomed to the process of writing a research paper for academic courses. To this end, the process of composing the paper has been divided into steps, with specific assignment instructions for each. This approach makes the overall process less difficult and intimidating for students who have never before written a research paper. Students who are familiar with the process because they have written such papers in another language will find the information, assignments, and exercises a valuable guide to adapting to conventions and formats acceptable in English.

The book can be used in different ways: as part of a general writing course, in a course devoted entirely to writing a research paper, as a reference book for individual students, or as a supplementary text in academic courses in which students are required to write research papers.

SPECIAL FEATURES

The features that characterize this guide are

a steady insistence on the fact that the writing process is recursive, open-ended, and generative of ideas

simplicity of language of explanation wherever this is achievable without oversimplifying the concepts

the use of ESL peer models as an encouragement to ESL writers

cross-cultural awareness, reflected in careful explanation of culturally determined issues such as plagiarism an extensive glossary of terminology related to research paper writing and library use

These features and the use of a step by step approach will assist instructors in changing a potentially daunting and anxiety-ridden experience for their students into one that is manageable, interesting, and rewarding.

CHANGES IN THE REVISED EDITION

Since the publication of the first edition of *Writing a research paper,* computers have had a great impact on both composing and research processes. Changes have accordingly been made in this edition. Due to the availability of word processing software, there is no longer any need for research paper writers to rely on file cards for preliminary bibliography, note-taking, drafting, and revising. The assignments in this edition are set up so that either word processing or traditional approaches may be used. Another major change is that computerized database searching in libraries is allowed for, in addition to the use of traditional card catalogs and printed indexes.

In this new edition, the widely used APA style manual (*Publication manual of the American Psychological Association,* 4th ed., 1994) again provides the necessary editorial guidelines for formatting a research paper. Users of the first edition may notice that the chapter exemplifying MLA and scientific styles has been omitted in this edition. This has been done in the interest of keeping this volume brief and because the attempt to squeeze the two additional styles into one short chapter was not found to be helpful—too much was left out. However, at various points in the assignment instructions in this edition, students are invited to use, if they wish, any editorial style that they are familiar with or that may be required of them in their future studies. The appendix on page 140 lists several style guides and other resources.

ACKNOWLEDGMENTS

In the development of both editions of *Writing a research paper,* students and teachers in the University of Pittsburgh English Language Institute have made valuable suggestions for improvements of various kinds. I thank them, and I especially thank the many students who gave permission for their research paper work to be quoted as examples. The first edition of the book owed much to Mary N. Bruder and Christina B. Paulston, who encouraged its production. I am grateful to Cathy Cake, Lois Wilson, Christine O'Neill, Betsy Davis, and Jhon Smith for their very helpful advice for improving the new edition. The insightful ideas and eagle-eyed editorial work of the University of Michigan Press editors, Kelly Sippell and Andrea Olson, have contributed to making this a better textbook; their efforts are greatly appreciated. Finally, like all writers of educational materials, I am indebted to my own teachers: I learned much about the teaching of composition from Professors Anthony R. Petrosky, David Bartholomae, William L. Smith, and William E. Coles, all of the University of Pittsburgh.

TO THE TEACHER

The units that contribute directly to step by step production of a research paper are 2, 4, 5, 6, 7, 8, 10, 11, 12, 13, 14, and 15. Most of these units are divided into three parts:

Assignment Instruction ("RP Assignment")

Supporting Explanation

Examples

Exercises are included in some of these units.

Units 1, 3, 9, 16, 17, and 18 do not begin with an assignment instruction but provide essential information and/or exercises for understanding the nature and purpose of research papers, developing a bibliography, understanding and avoiding plagiarism, and creating a consistent and acceptable format for a paper in APA style.

The following general procedure has been found to work very well for class use of a typical unit:

1. Assign the unit to be read as homework.
2. If the unit begins with an RP Assignment instruction, read it aloud to the class. Mention the due date for the assignment. Discuss any assignment points that the students ask about. If the unit does not begin with an RP Assignment, it can still be read for homework and discussed in class.
3. Do some of the exercises in the unit, either in class or partly in class and partly as homework. It is not necessary to do all the exercises with all students; instructors should select those that will be most useful for each particular group of students.
4. Have the students complete the RP Assignment for homework by the due date.
5. Check or grade the completed assignments in relation to how well they contribute to the overall research paper writing process. Points may be assigned to each step to ensure that student effort is distributed evenly over the whole process.

WORLD WIDE WEB SITE

There is a World Wide Web site associated with this textbook:

http://www.linguistics.pitt.edu/~lion/wrp.html

Here, teachers may access and freely use additional exercises for students, as well as other support material for instruction (such as a research paper grading sheet and a typical term schedule). Teachers can communicate with the author by e-mail via the site. Suggestions, comments and hints from teachers are welcome and may be displayed at the site.

Contents

Each of the twelve units in *italics* begins with an assignment instruction that is part of the sequence building up into a complete research paper.

Unit 1
Writing Research Papers

An extremely common requirement of many academic courses is the *research paper* or *term paper*. It is a lengthy written composition that is usually developed and written during the course of a whole term or semester. In essence, it involves the writer in searching for published information on a specific topic, studying and thinking about this information, and then writing about the topic in a way that makes use of the information.

It is an activity that many ESL students are not familiar with, and most are not familiar with the English language conventions that are involved, even when they have written such papers in their own languages. All this unfamiliarity causes anxiety and stress in students beginning programs in which many such papers will be demanded of them. If you are just such a student, you should not feel that the task is too much for you. In fact, the process of producing a good research paper is not really very difficult to understand and control if you practice it in small steps and stages. What follows in this and subsequent units is the step by step practice that will provide you with understanding of the process and confidence in your ability to write good, even excellent, research papers.

As you work on your research papers, bear in mind why they are a standard scholarly activity: they demonstrate that the writer has read widely in a certain subject area (implying familiarity with library resources), assimilated and thought critically about the reading, and, finally, written a fully documented exposition of the issues.

TYPES OF RESEARCH PAPERS

In its broadest sense, the term *research* simply means scholarly or scientific investigation or inquiry. When applied to a student's work for a particular paper, the term can mean one of two things:

1. **Report research paper.** A writer may gather information on a topic from several sources and present it in paraphrase (i.e., in his or her own words) in a coherent, organized way. In this type of paper, the writer reports what others have said without making any attempt to add personal comments, or a personal point of view, on the main issue. This is a common requirement of undergraduate courses and is often called a *report*.

2. **Argumentative research paper.** When the writer presents the ideas of others and also makes judgments on them, adds personal comments, and tries to support a different, personal position on the main issue, the paper is an argumentative one. (It is sometimes called a *thesis*.) In graduate courses, this is the standard requirement. This is also the type of paper that scholars publish in journals because it is this type that communicates advances in knowledge, new ideas, and new points of view. Sometimes this type of paper forms the basis of a proposal (as for a graduate thesis or dissertation) because it concludes with a statement of a proposed project that the writer or someone else will undertake.

STEPS IN WRITING A RESEARCH PAPER

A look at the contents page of this book will give you a general idea of some of the stages you must go through in producing a research paper. The following flowchart will give you a more detailed picture.

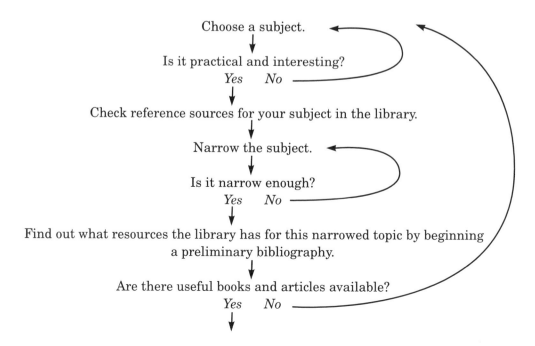

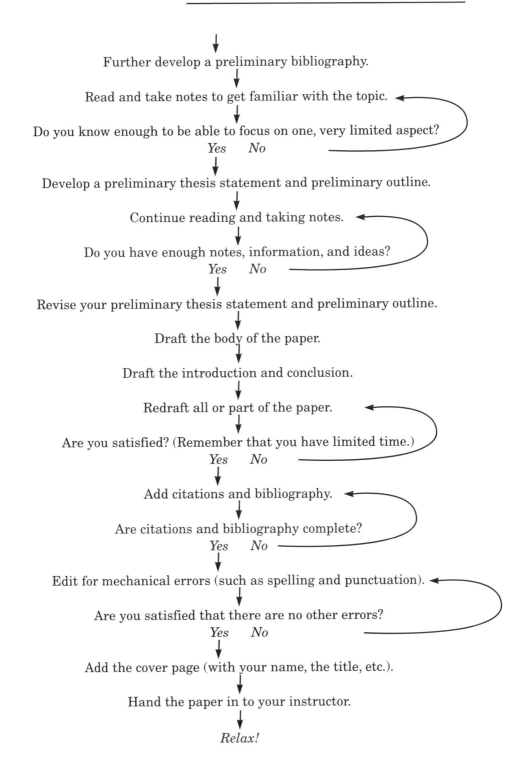

Further develop a preliminary bibliography.

Read and take notes to get familiar with the topic.

Do you know enough to be able to focus on one, very limited aspect?
Yes   No

Develop a preliminary thesis statement and preliminary outline.

Continue reading and taking notes.

Do you have enough notes, information, and ideas?
Yes   No

Revise your preliminary thesis statement and preliminary outline.

Draft the body of the paper.

Draft the introduction and conclusion.

Redraft all or part of the paper.

Are you satisfied? (Remember that you have limited time.)
Yes   No

Add citations and bibliography.

Are citations and bibliography complete?
Yes   No

Edit for mechanical errors (such as spelling and punctuation).

Are you satisfied that there are no other errors?
Yes   No

Add the cover page (with your name, the title, etc.).

Hand the paper in to your instructor.

Relax!

The sequence shown in this chart may seem quite complicated, but if you think about each step separately and concentrate on that step alone, you will be surprised at how you get through it all quite easily. Do not think too much about the final product or about the whole process that takes so many weeks or months. Certainly you should keep these in mind in a general way, so that you know where you are going and how you will get there, but concentrate on each step separately as you go along, and your research paper writing will not be so difficult after all.

THE STRUCTURE OF RESEARCH PAPERS

Regardless of subject area, most research papers have a similar general structure. The *introductory paragraphs* state what is to be discussed and give the context of the subject, normally mentioning work done by others. The introduction then usually mentions how the writer will deal with the subject, whether by summarizing and synthesizing the work of others (a report), or by arguing logically about facts and theories, or by presenting the results of experimental research, or in any other way or combination of ways. The end of the introduction usually includes the main idea sentence (or thesis statement).

The longest section of a research paper is usually called the *body* to distinguish it from the introduction and conclusion. It consists of many paragraphs, carefully linked with the introduction and conclusion and with each other, which present information and discussion in an organized way.

The *concluding paragraphs* usually summarize the main points of the paper and restate, in different wording, the thesis statement. Often the conclusion also has some indication of the implications and consequences of the study, such as a recommendation for action or further research.

Unit 2
Choosing a Subject

RP Assignment

Choosing a Subject

Decide on a subject that you want to write about, but at this first stage do not narrow it down too much. Make a note of it on a sheet of paper and add a few sentences explaining why you want to work on this particular subject. Hand it in to your instructor by the due date.

There are two guiding principles to remember when choosing something to write about: practicality and interest.

Being practical about your choice means that you must consider the available time and the published resources on your topic. Because you have a limited time to work in, you must be sure that there will be adequate information immediately available to you in your college library or from local libraries and information sources. This is usually not a problem for most students in selecting a subject. If you are taking a course in biology, for instance, the general subject area will usually be well represented in the libraries. If the course is a more specialized one within biology, in cell biology or lipids, for example, there will still be basic reference materials available in most libraries. However, when the subject area is not dictated by the course, there may be a problem: your topic may be too unusual or too specialized for your school and public libraries. Quite often ESL students choose to write about their home countries, perhaps their histories or education systems, but the libraries may or may not have useful materials for these topics. If you are considering writing about some aspect of your home country, you should not assume that there will be enough information available locally. A preliminary survey of local resources is very essential in such a case.

Interest, as well as practicality, is important in topic selection because you will be working with this subject for many weeks. If you do not have a real interest in it, you may lose motivation later, and this will make your task much harder. A common and realistic question students frequently ask at this stage is, "How will I know that I can maintain interest in the subject until I have studied it thoroughly? It seems that I must already have studied the subject in order to know if I want to study it!" There is no simple answer to this question. There is indeed some risk in choosing a subject area you have not studied before. However, one of the aims of the research paper is to provide an opportunity for you to gain a deep understanding of a subject. So you can think positively about either approach: a familiar subject will enable you to explore special aspects of it in more depth, while an unfamiliar subject lets you discover new areas of knowledge. Even with an unfamiliar subject, most researchers usually find that the more they get into it, the more interesting it becomes.

In general, you should try to select something that seems to promise real value to you, perhaps something that you have always wanted to learn more about but have lacked the opportunity to study, or possibly a subject that you know will be valuable to you later in your more specialized academic work.

Examples: Choosing a subject

Example **1.** (Fumiaki Ito)
Topic: The automobile industries in Japan and the United States.
I have been interested in this since I came here to the United States. The relationship between these two countries' automobile industries is complicated, and they are in competition.

Example **2.** (Ghareeb Ghareeb)
The topic is an investigation of the relationship between depression and assertiveness. I have chosen this topic because I will use it for my dissertation, and it is something that interests me.

Example ➤ **3.** (Synian Hwang)

Topic: In the subject area of statistics—some aspects of the theoretical developments in the sampling theorem.

Explanation of choice: I am interested in the subject.

Example ➤ **4.** (Boshin Lin)

Topic: Computer applications in Biological Science.

Why? Because my college major was Biology and now I am majoring in Information Science, which uses the computer as a basic tool. I have chosen this topic, hoping it will relate these two majors.

Example ➤ **5.** (Elizabeth Kiener)

Topic: A comparison between Swiss and United States schools.

Explanation of choice: My children had to adjust to the U.S. schools, in which the discipline seems stricter and the results not better.

Example ➤ **6.** (Dagmar Kamecke)

Topic: Recycling

I have chosen this because I am interested in environmental questions, but unfortunately, during my studies of economics, I have lacked the opportunity to analyze this kind of problem. Recycling is one important means to avoid or reduce garbage, and I am curious about its possibilities and limitations.

Unit 3
Using the Library

If you have never written a research paper before, you may be surprised at how much time you spend in the library finding relevant and useful materials. You will move many times between the catalog, the reference area, the indexes, the book stacks, the periodicals room, and possibly the microform readers. You will also have to consult the librarians a number of times. The process may seem complicated at first, but all it takes to become familiar with a library is some practice.

Your instructor or a librarian may give you an orientation tour of the library, but after that you should never hesitate to ask one of them for help. As an information sheet for students in one university library puts it:

> Do not be afraid to ask for help. While the Reference Librarians will not choose a topic for you, or determine which aspect of a topic you should explore, they will help you to identify your interest and to select opening sets of terms. If you are unsure about how to choose, narrow, and refine your topic; if you are not sure where to begin or how to proceed; if you do not understand the organization of a source (e.g., catalog, bibliography, index, etc.), or the meaning of certain symbols or abbreviations, ASK A REFERENCE LIBRARIAN. Try them. You'll like them!

Do not expect that all your walking about in the library will always lead you to the books and articles you are looking for. Part of the initial research activity is almost always frustration at not finding what you want. Keep on looking until you are certain that the materials are not available for your topic and only then consider changing to a topic for which information is more easily available.

A BASIC LIBRARY RESEARCH STRATEGY

A typical strategy for beginning to work in the library includes the following three steps (more detail will be given on this in unit 5):

1. When you have selected a topic, try to get general background knowledge by reading an encyclopedia entry about it. Aim to find some **key words** or **key phrases**, called *search terms,* for your later subject searching of catalogs and indexes.

2. Look for **books** by subject, author, or title. Start searching for them in library catalogs. Make use of the *Library of Congress Subject Headings* (if your library uses this classification system) to help you find appropriate search terms.

3. Look for **periodical articles** by subject or author. Start searching for them in printed or computerized indexes.

LIBRARY OF CONGRESS CALL NUMBER

Each book in the library is assigned a **call number**; this is the number that is written on the spine of the book. In a catalog, it is shown prominently because it is the number you use in order to locate the book on the library shelves.

The Library of Congress classification system and the Dewey Decimal system are the most common types of numbering. The Library of Congress system is the most used one in college and university libraries, and so it is the one discussed here.

An example of a call number is P105. V996. 1962. This is for the book *Thought and Language* by L. S. Vygotsky. The numbers have the following meanings:

> P105   class number
> V996   author number
> 1962   date of publication

Here, the P stands for the general subject area (in this case, Language and Literature), and the 105 is a sequence of numbers for further subdivisions of the class number. Sometimes the class number starts with two letters, with the second letter referring to a subdivision of the subject. The V is the first part of the author number—also called the book number. This usually starts with the first letter of the author's last name (in this instance, Vygotsky), and this letter is followed by a number sequence for further subdivision of the book category. The third line in this example is the date of this edition of the book (in this case, 1962). When you are looking for books, you must be sure to copy out exactly the whole call number, keeping the letters and numbers in the right order.

To find a book, follow these steps:

1. Start on the left of the class number to find the area of the library shelves where books with the first letter are located.

2. Work from left to right. If there is then another letter, find its shelf location within the area indicated by the first letter.

3. Then work from left to right with the numerals to locate the area of each numeral in turn. The numerals, referring to subsections of subject areas, become more specific as you work through them.

4. Next, move to the book (author) number. Again work from left to right, taking each letter and numeral in turn, one at a time. Again, you will be getting more and more specific, and, if the book is on the shelf (not out on loan and not out of position), you should find it when you reach the last numeral.

Note also:

(a) If you see a small letter q or f before the class number, this means that the book is a larger size ("quarto" or "folio") and is in a different section of the library. Ask a librarian about the location.

(b) Sometimes, after the author number or date, you will see a small letter c with a number following it. This simply means "copy" and refers to how many copies are in the library (for example, "c2" means "second copy").

(c) Sometimes, for extra subdivision, the class number has two lines, or the author number has an extra letter among the numerals, or a line has a decimal point in it.

The following library exercises will give you practice in different aspects of library use. Do them as directed by your instructor—some in class, some for homework, and most of them in the library.

Exercises: Using the library

(Numbers 1–5 can be done in class.)

Exercise 1

Choose any two or three books that you have in class or that your teacher brings to class. Study their title pages and copyright pages in order to find, for each book, the name of the author, full title, year of publication, and publisher.

Exercise 2

Study the following example of an entry in a computerized catalog. Answer these questions:

(a) What is the author's name?

(b) What is the title of the book?

(c) When was it published?

(d) Who published the book?

(e) What is its call number?

```
Search Request: T=BOOK OF JAMAICA
University of Pittsburgh
BOOK - Record 1 of 1 Entry Found
Brief View

_____

TITLE: The book of Jamaica / Russell Banks.

AUTHOR: Banks, Russell, 1940-

EDITION: 1st HarperPerennial ed.

PUBLISHED: New York : HarperPerennial, 1996.

DESCRIPTION:  336 p. ; 21 cm.
```

```
LOCATION:   CALL NUMBER          STATUS:
HILLMAN     PS3552 A49B6 1996 Not checked out
LIB-AFRO-AMERICAN
(1st fl)


                    Page 1 of 1


STArt over          LONg view
HELp
OTHer options


NEXTCOMMAND:
```

Exercise 3

(a) Alphabetize the family names of all the students in your class.

(b) Alphabetize the following names according to family names. Write each one with the family name first, followed by a comma and then the first name(s). For example, the name *Peter R. Johnson* would be written *Johnson, Peter R.* in your list. Note these points before you begin:

In English the last name that you see written is generally the family name.

In some Asian names, the family name is written first, and so the first name that you see written is the one to use for alphabetization purposes.

When two last names are the same, use the first name's initials for further alphabetization.

In this exercise, when the parts of a name are joined by a hyphen or an apostrophe, and when the last name includes separate elements such as "van der," "von," "de," "el," "al," treat these elements as part of the last name. (However, there is a lot of variation in the way libraries treat these names. When searching for references in a library, look under both parts of the last name if you cannot find a reference where you expect it to be.)

Names to alphabetize:

Thomas Lee Crowell, Helen Barnard, Carol Washington Pollock, Marcella Frank, Robert G. Bander, Edward T. Hall, George Orwell, Alan T. Hall, Frank d'Angelo, Ali el-Osman, Hendrik van der Merwe, Heinz von Loring, Albert Peter Hall, Ahmed al-Arabi, Pierre de Proyart, Jaime de los Rios, John Smith, James R. Smith, Xavier Ortega, Wang Minn-Hu, Matsushita Yoko, P. R. O'Hara, F. Williams, P. George Zelman, JoEllen Walker, Hamish Angus McTaggart

Exercise 4

Look at this call number and answer the questions that follow it.

BV5077
R9
F2
1978
c14

(a) What is the general subject area represented by the letter B? (Refer to the glossary at the end of this textbook; look under "Library of Congress Subject Headings.")

(b) The author's name is Fedotov. Which line is the author number?

(c) Do you think this is the first edition of this book?

(d) The library has many copies of this book. At least how many do you think it has?

Exercise 5A

Study the following examples of records from a computerized index, *PsycLIT*. Answer the questions that follow.

Record 5 of 15 in PsycLIT Journal Archives 1/90–9/96
DOCUMENT TITLE
    Combined dance/movement, art, and music therapies with a developmentally de-
layed, psychiatric client in a day treatment setting.
AUTHOR(S)
    Zagelbaum,-Valorie-N.; Rubino,-Maria-A.
INSTITUTIONAL AFFILIATION OF FIRST AUTHOR
    Meadowbrook Manor, CA, US
JOURNAL NAME
    Arts-in-Psychotherapy;1991 Vol 18(2) 139–148;
PSYC ABS. VOL. AND ABS. NO.
    78-28090

Record 6 of 15 in PsycLIT Journal Archives 1/90–9/96
DOCUMENT TITLE
    Social skill self-assessments by adolescents with hearing impairment in residen-
tial and public schools.
AUTHOR(S)
    Cartledge,-Gwendolyn; Cochran,-Lessie; Paul,-Peter
INSTITUTIONAL AFFILIATION OF FIRST AUTHOR
    Ohio State U, Dept of Education, Columbus, OH US
JOURNAL NAME
    Remedial-and-Special-Education;1996 Jan Vol 17(1) 30–36;
PSYC ABS. VOL. AND ABS. NO.
    83-28714

---

1. What is the title of the article that Maria A. Rubino coauthored?

2. What is the name of the journal in which G. Cartledge, L. Cochran, and P. Paul published an article?

3. In which issue of *Arts in Psychotherapy*, and on what pages, is the article "Combined dance/movement, art, and music therapies with a developmentally delayed, psychiatric client in a day treatment setting"?

4. What is the abstract volume and number in *PsycLIT* of the article titled "Social skill self-assessments by adolescents with hearing impairment in residential and public schools"?

Exercise 5B

Study the following extract from the printed index *Readers' Guide to Periodical Literature*. Answer the questions that follow.

LIBERAL-DEMOCRATIC PARTY (JAPAN)
    In Japan, the LDP wins—and the economy loses. B. Bremner. il por *Business Week* p79
      N 4 '96
    Why Japan Inc. is turning its back on the politicians. B. Bremner. il *Business Week* p64
      O 14 '96
LIBERAL PARTY (CANADA)
    The Liberals' best hope. A. Wilson-Smith. il *Maclean's* v109 p19 Je 24 '96
LIBERALISM
    Bad terms [reasons not to vote for B. Clinton] R. Steel. *The New Republic* v215 p21 O
      21 '96
    Down with compassion [liberal moralism] E. Willis. *The New Yorker* v72 p4-5 S 30 '96
    In the matter of the Court vs. Us [R. Bork alleges increasing liberalization of the Su-
      preme Court] J. Leo. il *U.S. News & World Report* v121 p28 O 7 '96
    Left turn ahead: up from liberalism: the emerging contours of a new progressivism. D.
      D. Kallick. *The Nation* v263 p22-4 N 11 '96
    Liberalism and the culture: a turning of the tide? [cover story] N. Podhoretz. *Commen-
      tary* v102 p25-32 O '96
    Liberals, R.I.P. [editorial] *The Progressive* v60 p10 O '96
    Middle march [post-liberal Democrats fight for the House] J. B. Judis. *The New Repub-
      lic* v215 p18-20 O 21 '96
    The myth of the liberal media. B. Nussbaum. il *Business Week* p34-5 N 11 '96
    No holiday for the busman [P. D. Wellstone's Senate race in Minn.] D. Corn. il *The
      Nation* v263 p15-16+ O 21 '96
LIBERALISM (RELIGION)
    Of dinosaurs, carrier pigeons and disappearing priests. R. E. Schmitz. il *America* v175
      p7-8+ O 12 '96
LIBERIA

History
Civil War. 1989-

    History and hope. D. Olson. il *The Christian Century* v113 p294-6 O 9 '96

---

1. Name the author of an article titled "History and hope."

2. In which publication, dated October 14, 1996, did B. Bremner write an article?

3. In Volume 263 of *The Nation,* there is an article titled "Left turn ahead: Up from liberalism: The emerging contours of a new progressivism." On what pages does this article appear?

4. What is the title of an article by B. Nussbaum?

5. In what volume number of *The New Yorker* is there an article by E. Willis?

6. Under what subject heading is the article titled "The Liberal's best hope"?

7. Is the article by R. E. Schmitz in *America* illustrated?

8. In which issue of *The Progressive* is there an editorial titled "Liberals, R.I.P."?

Exercise 6

Choose one of the following authors: Pablo Neruda, William Shakespeare, Kahlil Gibran.

(a) Look in the catalog to see which of this author's works are available in the library. Remember that they are all alphabetized by author's last name.

(b) Note the call numbers of one or two of the writer's works and be sure that you know where to find them on the library shelves. Write down and hand in to your instructor the author's name, the title(s), and the call number(s).

If the books you are looking for are not on the shelves, where are they? A computerized catalog may tell you that the book is "charged out" (meaning someone has borrowed it) or "on reserve" (not to be borrowed, but kept in an area of the library where many students can read it). You may also get such information from a librarian.

Exercise 7

Locate the reference section in the library. Find two different sets of multivolume encyclopedias (such as *World Book Encyclopedia* or *Encyclopaedia Britannica*). Compare each one's entries on the same subject (such as your country or your city). Is there a bibliography at the end of each entry? If so, select one book from it and check in the catalog to see whether the library has it. If the library does not have it, try to find one of the listed books that is available in the library.

Exercise 8

Use the catalog subject entries to find out if the library has any books on one or two of the following subjects:

gemstones

solar energy

heart transplants

twins

Spanish poetry

digital electronics

impressionist art

Bali

spices

U.S. relations with Africa

Hawaii

biogenetic engineering

language teaching

Notice whether the information includes the terms *See* or *See also* followed by an extra reference. If so, follow up this cross-reference by looking for it too in the catalog.

Exercise 9

Locate the index *Readers' Guide to Periodical Literature*. Find an entry for one article on any subject that interests you. (Note that this does not ask you to find a subject entry, but only an entry for one **article** in a periodical.) Copy down the entry exactly as it appears. Then rewrite it without using any abbreviations at all. For this you will have to refer to the explanation of abbreviations at the front of each volume. (For example, you will find that "D" is the abbreviation of "December.")

Exercise 10

Find any specialized index for a subject that you are interested in. Select an entry for one article. Then make sure that you understand all the abbreviations. Refer to the explanation of abbreviations at the beginning of the index.

Exercise 11

For one article in *Readers' Guide to Periodical Literature* and for one in any other, more specialized index, note the following information:

author _____

title _____

name of journal (periodical) _____

volume number _____

page numbers _____

date of publication _____

Exercise 12

For both of the periodicals you noted in Exercise 11:

(a) Determine whether your library has them. To do so, consult the catalog under the name of the periodical.

(b) If they are available in the library, find their locations.

(c) When you find the periodicals, look for the articles you noted in Exercise 11. To do this, you need to use the volume number, year of publication, and page numbers of the article.

(d) Look at the end of each article. There you may find a bibliography that you can use for further references on the same topic. Is there one?

Exercise 13

If your library has both a card catalog and a computerized catalog of its books, do the following: For one book title, compare the catalog entries in each type of catalog. Is the information different in each and, if so, in what way?

Exercise 14

If your library has both card and computerized indexes for special subject areas, do the following: Find one *print* index that is of special interest to you and check to see if it is also in a computerized database. If so, compare the information given in each.

Unit 4
Narrowing the Focus

RP Assignment

Narrowing the Focus

Work out which specific aspect of your subject area you will investigate and write about. That is, narrow down or limit the focus of interest from a general subject to a specific topic. Make a note of this limited topic on a sheet of paper and hand it in to your instructor. Add a few sentences explaining how you have narrowed it down. To make this last point clear, contrast your narrowed topic with a broader one within the same subject area.

A suitably narrow or limited topic to do research on is always worked out after very careful thought. Unless you are already very familiar with your subject, you will probably discover as you begin to do the research that you have not limited it enough. At this stage, however, this is not a problem. In fact, it is part of the interest of the activity: you undertake research to find out what you do not know, and part of the learning is to discover how much has already been written on your topic.

To limit your topic, first survey what has so far been published. Note the different issues that are discussed. You will find that some are very general and others are more narrowly focused. Then, ask yourself whether you could select one of the issues discussed in these publications as the topic of your paper. You may find that some of the authorities on the subject disagree with each other on certain points. If so, these points, or one of them, may provide you with a topic to pursue further since such disagreement can give you an opportunity to think about the arguments and evidence and take your own position on the issue.

Consider this example: A student of African history may start out with the history of British colonialism as a general subject area. After a little reading in this area, the subject could be narrowed down to research on why the British gradually withdrew from their African colonies during the last fifty years. After further reading, the same subject could be limited even more, possibly to a study of one or two countries. Even further restriction of the subject could be necessary. For example, historians may disagree about why the British withdrew from their African colonies—and so the research paper writer may decide to investigate which of these historians' theories seems to provide the best explanation in regard to only one country.

Examples: Narrowing the focus of a subject

Example ▷ **1.** (Fumiaki Ito)
Narrowed topic: The economic relationship between the automobile industries in Japan and the United States

I will concentrate on how they have affected each other's sales recently and why they have affected each other. I will study the difference between the Japanese industry's point of view and the American one.

Example ▷ **2.** (Ghareeb Ghareeb)
My narrowed topic is an investigation of the relationship between depression and assertiveness in an Eastern population.

Depression and assertiveness are both subjects that have been researched. Recently the relationship between depression and assertiveness in Western culture has been confirmed. I am going to research the same relationship between the two variables in an Eastern culture. The purpose of the study is to find out the kind of relationship that exists between depression and assertiveness in an Egyptian population.

Example ▷ **3.** (Synian Hwang)
Narrowed topic: Some aspects of theoretical developments in the sampling theorem under the finite population model

Since the sampling theorem is too broad, I will concentrate my attention on the finite population model. Under this model, I will study some results from a theoretical point of view.

Example ▶ **4.** (Yehuda Beneduardo)
Narrowed topic: The use of audiovisual aids in language teaching

At first I thought of writing about the use of the language laboratory, but a lot has already been done on that, especially on the use of videotapes with audiotapes. So I will narrow it to a new experimental field, which is the use of microcomputers in a language laboratory, because there are some disagreements about how they can be used. Some people say that they are hard for students to use and still too expensive.

Example ▶ **5.** (Elizabeth Kiener)
My general subject was a comparison of Swiss and American schools, but since it is impossible to get references on Swiss schools in such a short time, I will mainly concentrate on U.S. schools. Only at specific points am I going to make comparisons to Swiss schools. I will focus on whether strict rules for classroom behavior encourage a humanistic school climate and/or self-discipline. I won't refer to punishments.

Example ▶ **6.** (Dagmar Kamecke)
The topic is the effectiveness of domestic plastic package recycling in the United States. Since there is a wide range of applications of plastic recycling, which includes the recycling of industrial plastics, and since these applications differ from country to country, I will concentrate on the plastic packages which are collected in the U.S. by households. With this narrowing, I can leave out detailed chemical explanations to focus on the economic and environmental aspects.

Exercises: Narrowing the focus of a subject

Exercise 1

Select one of the following general subjects and narrow it down in stages, becoming more and more specific at each stage, until you have limited it enough to be a suitable topic for a short research paper.

computers

hunting

card games

art

education

health

space travel

world languages

animals

biology

road building

Example

General subject: Health
Narrowed: Health maintenance
Narrowed further: Health maintenance in children
Narrowed further: Education for children about health maintenance
Narrowed further: Problems and solutions in educating children
                        about health maintenance
Narrowed further: The use of television cartoons as a means of
                        educating children about health maintenance
Narrowed further: The most effective type of television cartoon for
                        educating children about health maintenance

Exercise 2

Compare the two topics in each of the following pairs. Which one is narrower?

1. (a) Modern architecture in Europe
    (b) The beginnings of modern architecture in Europe

2. (a) Stage costumes in realist theater
    (b) Stage costumes in theatrical productions

3. (a) Evaluating the heart by electrocardiogram
    (b) The twenty-four-hour electrocardiogram

Exercise 3

For each group of three topics, decide which is the broadest and which is the narrowest. Be prepared to explain your choice.

1. (a) Discrimination against women in awarding sports scholarships
   (b) Types of sports scholarships
   (c) Women's and men's sports in colleges

   Broadest: _____
   Narrowest: _____

2. (a) Freedom of worship and presidential election campaigns
   (b) Religious issues and politics
   (c) Political campaigns and important religious issues

   Broadest: _____
   Narrowest: _____

3. (a) The artist's search for perfection
   (b) Achieving perfection in human activity
   (c) Musical rehearsals and perfecting orchestral performances

   Broadest: _____
   Narrowest: _____

Exercise 4

Select any general subject that you are interested in. Narrow it down stage by stage. Write down the subject and each stage of narrowing (as in the example in Exercise 1) to hand in to your instructor. Be sure that the final step is limited enough for a short research paper.

Unit 5

Finding Relevant Books and Articles

RP Assignment

List of Catalogs, Indexes, and Bibliographies

Go to the library (or to more than one library) and find out what catalogs, indexes, and bibliographies may help you to locate relevant books and articles on your topic. List the names of the catalogs, indexes, and bibliographies and hand the list in to your instructor.

Include the following in your list:
   The card catalog or computerized catalog
   Printed indexes or computerized indexes
   Bibliographies (or "References" lists) in books or
     articles

An essential step at the beginning of your research is to find out what sources will help you locate relevant books and articles in your subject area. Typically, these sources are catalogs, indexes, and bibliographies:

Catalogs are the lists of publications held by a library; they refer mostly to books; they may also include the names of journals (periodicals) held by the library.

Indexes give publication information (such as author, title, and date) for articles and books; they may be in printed or computerized (electronic) form.

Bibliographies (or **reference lists**) are lists of publications that authors have consulted or quoted; they are generally placed at the ends of books or articles (and sometimes at the end of each chapter in a book).

Your first stop in the library should be the catalog, where you should begin by looking up **subject headings** related to your research topic. If, in this way, you find too many book titles that seem relevant, you must use narrower **subheadings** for your search. Book titles themselves may give you a clue on ways to limit the search. **Cross-references** in the catalog may also lead you to related material under narrower subheadings.

As you proceed with this, make a note of all the words and short phrases that describe aspects of your subject. These will be your **search terms**—key words used as headings and subheadings in classifying subject areas. Different indexes may use slightly different terms (also called *descriptors*). You can also use the *Library of Congress Subject Classifications* as a source of search terms if your library uses this classification system. Copies of this four-volume publication are usually located near the catalog or at the library's reference desk.

Although you should start with the catalog, it is rarely enough as a source of information for useful references. It gives only the titles of books and the names of periodicals. It does not give you something that you must also have—the titles of articles.

In order to write an up-to-date paper, you will need to decide on what recent articles to read. To find out about these, you should look through indexes, both the general ones and those that are specific to your subject area. The reference librarians will help you find them. Often, one of the first general ones you are shown will be the *Readers' Guide to Periodical Literature,* which covers articles in the more popular magazines. Others of a more scholarly type might include, for example, the *Humanities Index* and *Social Science Index.*

If you do not know the specialized indexes for your subject, ask a librarian for the *Guide to Reference Books* (edited by Gordon Sheehy). This will help you discover relevant indexes and other reference materials. Another guide to finding such materials is the *Bibliographic Index,* which lists books and journal articles that have bibliographies. Also, it is now common for researchers to conduct computerized searches of bibliographic databases. Most large college libraries have such facilities, and the search is often free. Some computer searches provide abstracts (summaries of main points) of the articles, in addition to title, author, date, and other publication details.

Finally, it is important to remember that people, as well as books and computers, can be used to obtain bibliographic information. This is especially important for graduate students and is often the quickest way to find recent and useful articles and books. Approach the professors and advanced graduate students in your subject and ask them to refer you to recent books or survey articles. They will probably also be helpful in telling you about the relevant indexes in your field or about other ways of obtaining bibliographic information.

Once you are familiar with the materials that will lead you to relevant books and articles, you can begin to work on the next stage—the preparation of your own preliminary bibliography for your research paper. For this, you must return to the catalog to use it for another of its main functions—indicating by means of call numbers what books are located in the library.

SOME INDEXES FOR DIFFERENT SUBJECT AREAS

The following examples of indexes are just a small selection from the many available. A librarian can help you find the ones relevant to your research topic.

Anthropological Literature

Business Education Index

Business Periodicals Index

Biological Abstracts

Current Index to Journals in Education

Child Development Abstracts and Bibliography

Education Index

Humanities Index

International Political Science Abstracts

MLA International Bibliography of Books and Articles on the Modern Languages and Literatures

Psychological Abstracts

Readers' Guide to Periodical Literature

Social Sciences Index

Sociology: Review of Books

Urban Studies Abstracts

Some electronic indexes are

Applied Science & Technology Abstracts

Business and Company ASAP

EconLit

ERIC (Educational Resources Information Center)

Information Science Abstracts (ISA)

LegalTrac

MathSci Abstracts

MedLine Express

MLA Bibliography

PsycLIT

National Newspaper Index

SocioFile

Examples: Lists of catalogs, indexes, and bibliographies

The following are examples of lists prepared by students for their research papers. All begin with the library catalog since it is the usual starting point when searching for books. Some of the listed indexes are in print form, and others are on computerized databases.

Example 1. This list is for a research paper on a topic in electrophysiology. (Oris Calvo)

Library catalog

Biological Abstracts

Hospital Literature Index

Index Medicus

Science Citation Index

Van Nostrand's Scientific Encyclopedia

Bibliography from the following book: Chou, T. (1979). *Electrocardiography in clinical practice*. New York: Grune & Stratton.

Bibliography from the following article: Armstrong, W. F., et al. (1983). The S-T segment during ambulatory electrocardiographic monitoring. *Annals of Internal Medicine, 98*, 249–252.

Example 2. This list is for a research paper on modern architecture and politics. (Barbara Hoberman)

Library catalog

Art Index

Encyclopedia of World Art

Readers' Guide to Periodical Literature

Urban Studies Index

Abstracts of Popular Culture

Example 3. This list is for a research paper on a historical topic—the Knights Templars in Europe. (Maria Ricote)

Library catalog

Combined Retrospective Index to Journals in History

Expanded Academic Index

Folklore Studies

Historical Abstracts Index

Index to Religious Periodical Literature

Religion and Theological Abstracts

Reviews in European History

Example▶ 4. This list is for a research paper on second language learning. (Maria Moliterno)

Library catalog

Education Index

Language Teaching

Linguistics and Language Behavior Abstracts (LLBA)

New Encyclopaedia Britannica

Bibliography from the following book: Celce-Murcia, M. (Ed.). (1991). *Teaching English as a second or foreign language* (2nd ed.). New York: Newbury House.

Unit 6
Preliminary Bibliography

RP Assignment

Preliminary Bibliography

Prepare a preliminary bibliography for your research paper. This bibliography is a list of available books and articles that you think will be useful sources of information and ideas when writing the paper. For this assignment, do the following:

1. List at least ten items.
2. Include books and articles.
3. Alphabetize the list.
4. Note the call number for each book you find in a library.
5. At the beginning of your list, note which style guide you are following. If you follow the examples in this unit, write: *Style: APA.* If you decide to follow another guide, give your instructor a photocopied page showing a sample of the style you will use (some are listed in the Appendix on p. 140). Whichever style you choose, *be consistent:* follow *only* that style in *all* your research paper documentation.

For a **book,** you must note the following: author, title, date, publisher, and place of publication.

For an **article,** note these items: author, title of article, title of journal, volume number and/or issue number, and page numbers of the article.

Write down *all* the information about the publication because it will save you time later, especially if you want to include it in your final reference list. You would not want to find, as the due date for the asssignment gets closer, that you forgot to note the name of the publisher or the date of publication; then you would have to search for the same publication information again. Similarly, you can save time and avoid later frustration by carefully following the format of a style guide at this early stage. As the deadline for handing in your paper draws nearer, you will be concerned with its content rather than the mechanics of the citation format.

THE PROCESS OF DEVELOPING THE LIST

To prepare a preliminary bibliography you must work in the library with the indexes relevant to your field and with the catalog. You can also get ideas for this preliminary list from the references and bibliographies given in books and articles that are closely connected with your topic.

The preparation of this list is an ongoing process. Once you begin to read for information in the material that you find, you will come across other references. However, at the very beginning of the search for information, you should simply list whatever may seem relevant. Then, when you have an initial ten or so items on your list, check to see whether they are locally available. At this point in the process, you should try to find the items in the main college libraries, on the shelves, to ensure that they are available. Many of the relevant references may not be held by the library, others may be lost, and others may be out on loan and difficult to get back in time for you to use. When you do find some of the items, take a quick look at their bibliographies to see if they yield further titles for your search; if so, follow those up too. You do not need to begin the detailed reading of your books and articles at this point, but it is necessary to skim the material very quickly to be sure that it is relevant to your topic.

Expect to spend several hours going back and forth between the indexes, catalogs, shelves, and, if necessary (it normally is necessary for researchers), the librarians, who will help when something is difficult for you to find. If something is listed in the catalog, it should be either in the library or out on loan; if not, consult the librarian. Some libraries maintain a computerized list of what is out on loan. You can usually consult such lists without first asking a librarian.

Sometimes you will find that your initial judgment of what seemed useful is wrong, because you at first were able to judge only from the title or an abstract (a summary of the content of a book or an article). Items that you quickly skim and find irrelevant should not be included in the preliminary bibliography that you give to your instructor; it should contain only those items definitely relevant and available to you. Remember that it is not necessarily the case that something will be available just because it is in the catalog; you must ensure that it is actually there by checking the shelves.

When you begin to look in the catalog and in journal indexes for references, you may find that there are a very large number of them related to your topic. In such a situation, it is certainly the case that your topic is still not narrow enough. For the limited time available for a student paper, you must have a topic that is extremely limited in range. One approximate indication that it is really limited enough is that you will find only a few references directly related to your topic, although there may be many that are indirectly related.

File Cards as an Alternative

If you are handwriting your list or using a manual typewriter, you should consider writing each item of the bibliography on a separate card and not as a list on a sheet of paper. A file card system is useful because it is convenient when adding and removing items and when alphabetizing. In the end, it can save you a lot of time.

FORMAT OF REFERENCES IN APA STYLE

The rules and examples that follow are based on the style of the *Publication Manual of the American Psychological Association,* 4th ed. (1994), which is widely used in the social sciences, in education, and in many other fields. Its long title is often abbreviated to *Publication Manual* or *APA Manual,* and the style is referred to, for convenience, as "APA style."

What you will find in this and other chapters of this textbook is basic information that is adequate for most student term papers. However, if you have to cite an unusual type of source, or if you are writing a master's thesis or doctoral dissertation, you need to consult the detailed guidelines in the *Publication Manual* itself.

Electronic Publications

The increasing number of electronic publications (Internet journals, CD-ROM, etc.) is commented on as follows in the *APA Manual:* "At the time of writing this edition, a standard had not yet emerged for referencing on-line material. As with any published reference, the goals of an electronic reference are to credit the author and to enable the reader to find the material" (1994, p. 218). For your research paper, you should place the publication details for electronic references at the end of the entry after the word *Available,* as in the examples that follow. The *Publication Manual* provides some models for citing electronic media.

Remember that different subject areas have different conventions, which change as technology continues to develop. Therefore, when writing for academic courses, you should be sure to find out what is current in your subject area and follow the required format.

Books and Articles

There are four main parts to every reference citation:

1. author

2. date

3. title

4. publication details

There is no need to memorize the formats because you can always refer to examples if you forget them.

For the majority of students, most of the research paper citations will be of books and articles.

A standard **book citation** is in this order:

author's name

date of publication

book title

place of publication

publisher

A standard **article citation** is in this order:

author's name

date of publication

title of article

title of journal

volume number

page numbers of the article

Study the following examples of book and article citations in APA style.

Example ▶ **Book reference**

> Kuhn, T. S. (1970). *The structure of scientific revolutions.* Chicago: University of Chicago Press.

1. Indent first line

2. Author's last name, first letter capitalized, followed by a comma

3. Initials of author's first and middle names, each followed by a period

4. Date of publication, in parentheses, followed by a period

5. Book title, underlined or in italics, first letter of first word capitalized, followed by a period

6. Place of publication, followed by a colon

7. Name of publisher, followed by a period

Example ▶ **Article reference**

> DeKeyser, R. M. (1995). Learning second language grammar rules: An experiment with a miniature linguistic system. *Studies in Second Language Acquisition, 17,* 379–410.

1. Indent first line

2. Author's last name, first letter capitalized, followed by a comma

3. Initials of author's first and middle names, each followed by a period
4. Date of publication, in parentheses, followed by a period
5. Title of article, first letter of first word capitalized (not underlined and not in italics), colon to introduce subtitle, first letter of subtitle capitalized, followed by a period
6. Title of journal, underlined or in italics
7. Volume number of journal, underlined or in italics, followed by a comma
8. Page numbers of article, followed by a period

Points to Note for APA Citations

Separate the four main parts of a citation (author, date, title, and publication details) with periods. Use commas within each part (except between place and publisher, where a colon is used). Extra information (such as edition number) is placed in parentheses.

A later edition of a book is indicated after the title, in parentheses, and is not underlined or italicized.

Indent the first line of an entry.

The last name (family name, surname) of each author is written before the initial(s).

Only the initials of the authors' and editors' first names are used, not the complete first names.

The year of publication is placed in parentheses. (Add the month only when a periodical has no volume number.)

The title of an article is not underlined, but the title of a periodical (journal, magazine) is underlined or in italics.

The volume number of a journal is underlined or in italics.

The title of a book is underlined or in italics.

Titles of books and articles in reference lists are not capitalized throughout. Capitalize only the first letter of the first word, the first letter of the first word after a colon, and the first letter of a proper name.

In the title of a journal, capitalize the first letter of the first word and the first letter of each major word. (Do not capitalize short prepositions, conjunctions, or articles, except when one is the first word of the journal's title.)

When no author is given for a book or article, start with the title when alphabetizing.

An encyclopedia article is cited in the same way as an article in an edited book.

When there is a corporate author or editor (such as a committee or an association), put the name of the corporate author or editor in author position for alphabetization purposes.

Abbreviate the full name of the publishing company as much as possible by omitting initials and words such as *company* or *corporation*. (For example, write only "Norton" instead of "W. W. Norton and Company.")

Instead of *and,* use the symbol "&" between names of authors.

EXAMPLES IN APA STYLE

The examples that follow show the types of citation most often needed for student term papers. For other types, consult the *APA Manual*.

Book
Stuckey, S. (1994). *Going through the storm: The influence of African American art in history.* New York: Oxford University Press.

Book: Two authors
Brett, A., & Provenzo, E. F. (1995). *Adaptive technology for special human needs.* Albany, NY: State University of New York Press.

Book: Many authors
Moran, T. E., Levy, R., McClure, A., & Guthrie, J. L. (1997). *Evaluating transformation processes in municipal organizations.* New York: Center for Social Inquiry.

Book: Later edition
Brockett, O. G. (1992). *The essential theatre* (5th ed.). Fort Worth, TX: Harcourt Brace Jovanovich.

Book: Group author, same publisher as author
Motor Vehicle Manufacturer's Association of the United States. (1982). *World motor vehicle data.* Detroit, MI: Author.

Book: Edited
Ming, T., Tohen, M., & Zahner, M. E. P. (Eds.). (1995). *Textbook in psychiatric epidemiology.* New York: Wiley-Liss.

Book: Translated into English
Calvino, I. 1997. *The baron in the trees* (A. Colquhoun, Trans.). San Diego: Harcourt Brace Jovanovich. (Original work published 1959)

Book: Non-English
Walter, H. (1994). *L'aventure des langues en Occident: Leur origine, leur histoire, leur geographie* [The adventure of language in the West: Their origin, their history, their geography]. Paris: Editions Robert Laffont.

Article in journal
Maldonado, N. S. (1992). Making TV environmentally safe for children. *Childhood Education, 68,* 229-230.

Article in monthly magazine
Callihan, D. (1995, September). Through the window of pain. *Pitt Magazine, 10,* 20-23.

Article in weekly magazine: No author, one page
Dreams of roads and railways. (1995, March 11). *The Economist,* p. 48.

Article in edited book
Garcia, G. E., & Pearson, P. D. (1994). Assessment and diversity. In L. Darling-Hammond (Ed.), *Review of research in education* (pp. 337-391). Washington, DC: American Education Research Association.

Article in daily newspaper: No author, discontinuous pages
New bank attracts depositors with high rates. (1996, June 22). *Edinboro Gazette,* pp. 1, 5.

Conference paper: Published in conference proceedings
Barclay, L. P., Bateson, R., & Obiakor, T. F. (1996). Making computers talk. In P. R. Wigmore (Ed.), *Proceedings of the Second International Conference on Artificial Intelligence* (pp. 135-141). Amsterdam: De Bruijn Press.

Conference paper: Unpublished

Jameson, P. E. (1997, January). *Light filters in high-speed medical photography.* Paper presented at the meeting of the California Association of Medical Photography Technicians, Sacramento, CA.

Doctoral dissertation: Unpublished

Juffs, A. (1993). *Learnability and the lexicon: Chinese learners' acquisition of English argument structure.* Unpublished doctoral dissertation, McGill University, Montreal, Canada.

Report: Group author

Council for Exceptional Children Advocacy and Governmental Relations Committee. (1988). *Report of the Council for Exceptional Children's ad hoc committee on medically fragile students.* Reston, VA: CEC.

Review of a book

Forman, P. (1995). Truth and objectivity. [Review of the book *A social history of truth*] *Science, 269,* 707-710.

Electronic Publications

Note 1: There is no period at end of the entry because periods are part of electronic addresses; adding a final period would confuse the reader.

Note 2: If you want to, you may the add date of access [in brackets] at the end of an on-line entry, as in the first example that follows. This refers to the date on which you found the record through direct computer access.

World Wide Web: Article in electronic journal

Ling, R. (1996). Cyber McCarthyism: Witch hunts in the living room. *Electronic Journal of Sociology, 2.* Available: http://olympus.lang.arts.ualberta.ca:8010/vol002.001/Ling.Article.1996.html [1997, January 3]

World Wide Web: Article

Weaver, R., Servesco, R., & Tian, J. (1996). Determining the destiny of plastic. Available: http://dirac.py.iup.edu/college/chemistry/chemcourse/plastic.html

Internet: Article

Swaminathan, K. (1997). The limits of athletic endurance: A statistical model. Available: gopher://gopher.upr.edu/32/GH.research. unitphysiol.ftp

CD-ROM

Hille, T. (1996). *Form function in architecture,* [CD.ROM]. Available: University of Michigan Press.

Example ▶ Preliminary Bibliography

The following list was produced by a student in response to the assignment instruction at the beginning of this unit. Her general subject was student behavior in schools. She narrowed it down, first, to comparing school discipline in Switzerland and the United States, and then she narrowed it further to give more emphasis to the United States (as described in Unit 4, Example 5).

As the research process continues, the student will very probably add new references and remove some of those listed here.

Library call numbers (for example, LB 3011. B2) were noted by the student for some of the books and reports. Where there are no call numbers, either the reference is for a journal article or the student owns her own personal copy of the publication. (In the reference list for the final draft of the research paper, the call numbers are not included.)

Note: The type of reference [book, article, etc.] indicated here in brackets is for your information only; there is no need to add such labels to your bibliography for this assignment.

——————————————————————————

Elizabeth Kiener
Preliminary Bibliography for Research Paper (APA style)

Balson, M. (1982). *Understanding classroom behaviour.* Victoria, Australia: Australian Council for Educational Research.
LB 3011. B2

[book]

Galambos-Stone, J. (1978). *A guide to discipline.* Washington, DC: National Association for the Education of Young Children.

[book]

General Assistance Center on School Desegregation and Conflict. (1975). Creating a humanistic school climate. No place of publication. Eastern Pennsylvania 1975 Fall Workshop. Author.
qLB 3012. C73
[report of workshop, group author, no place of publication, publisher same as author]

Gilstrap, R. (1981). *Toward self-discipline.* Washington, DC: Association for Childhood Education International.
LB 3012. T68
[book]

Hill, D. (1995). The disciplinarian. *Education Week, 14,* 22-27.
[article]

Infante, D. A. (1995). Teaching students to understand and control verbal aggression. *Communication Education, 44,* 51-63.
[article]

Kohut, S. Jr., & Range, D. G. (1979). *Classroom discipline: Case studies and viewpoints.* Washington, DC: National Education Association.
LB 3013. T68
[book]

Leriche, L. (1992, January). The sociology of classroom discipline. *High School Journal,* 77-89.
[article, monthly publication, no volume number; month included with year]

Light, H. W., & Morrison, P. J. (1990). *Beyond retention.* Novato, CA: Academic Therapy Publications.
LB 3013. L52
[book]

Oggenfuss, A. (1988). Primary education in Switzerland. [Paper of Project No. 8 on "Innovation in primary education"] Strasbourg, France: Council for Cultural Co-Operation.
[paper published by an organization]

Pysch, R. (1991, December). Discipline improves as students take responsibility. *NASSP Bulletin,* 117-118.

> [article, monthly publication, no volume number; month included after year]

Rickover, H. G. (1962). *Swiss schools and ours: Why theirs are better.* No place of publication. Atlantic Monthly Press.
LA 931.8. R539

> [book, no place of publication]

Stone, G. L, & Lucas, J. (1994). Disciplinary counseling in higher education. *Journal of Counseling and Development, 72,* 234—238.

> [article]

— —

Exercises: Bibliographical Citations

Exercise 1

Together with other students in your class, write six references for some books and articles. The publications for this exercise may be brought to class by the instructor or students.

Exercise 2

Use the information in the following statements to write a complete citation for each book and article mentioned.

(a) Recently I came across a useful book called *Creating contexts for second language acquisition.* It was published by Longman and was written by Arnulfo G. Ramirez. It was published in 1995. The publisher is located in White Plains, in New York State.

(b) I strongly advise you to read that article in the *History of Applied Archaeology Quarterly.* Its author is a famous researcher named I. M. Inman. You'll find it between pages 119 and 123 in volume eighty-six. The title of the article is "Types of clay used in ancient Acapulcan pottery." It appeared in the journal in September 1934.

(c) I enjoyed reading a history of modern architecture that was written in 1992 by Kenneth Frampton. The title was *Modern architecture: A critical history.* It was published by Thames and Hudson, a company based in New York.

(d) Because of a 1992 article that I came across when I was writing my term paper, I changed the main idea of the paper; the article is entitled "Evreinov and Pirandello: Two theatricalists in search of the chief thing." It is on pages 130-136 of the journal *Theatre Survey,* in volume 32, and was written by T. Pearson.

Exercise 3

There is an error in each of the following citations. One thing is wrong in order of elements or punctuation or capitalization or underlining/ italics. Try to find what is wrong. Write out the corrected form or explain exactly how you would make it right.

(a)   Stein, H. (1995). "Economics of my time and yours." *Business Economics, 30,* 19-21.

(b)   Shimada, S. (Ed.). (1995). *Coherent lightwave communications technology.* Chapman and Hall: London.

(c)   Winston, P. H. (1985). Artificial intelligence. New York: Wesley.

(d)   Malik, M. (1990). Changes in the distribution of ventricular ectopic beats in long-term electrocardiograms. *Medical and Biological Engineering and Computing,* 28, 423-430.

(e)   Sadie, Stanley. (1990). *History of opera.* New York: Norton.

(f)   Haggard, A. A patient's best friend. (1985). *American Journal of Nursing, 85,* 1375-1376.

(g)   Wright, S. (1995). Language Planning and Policy-Making in Europe. *Language Teaching, 28,* 148-159.

Unit 7
Preliminary Thesis Statement

Preliminary Thesis Statement

Prepare a preliminary thesis statement for your research paper. It should express in one sentence the controlling idea of the whole paper.

For an argumentative paper, the thesis statement makes the claim that the paper tries to support with evidence.

For a report, the thesis statement does not make a claim that needs proof; instead, it is a statement describing the main idea, or it is a question that will be answered by the information given in the paper.

Write down your thesis statement and note in parentheses whether it is for an argumentative or a report paper.

Even though the thesis statement is only one sentence, it is very important and must be given a lot of thought because it expresses the main claim or main idea of the whole paper. The statement is called preliminary at this stage since you may find reason to change it as you proceed with your reading, note-taking, and drafting.

THESIS STATEMENT FOR AN ARGUMENTATIVE RESEARCH PAPER

To arrive at the thesis statement of an argumentative paper, you should first ask yourself: "What do I want to prove?" The answer to this question will express your main purpose in writing the paper and will therefore provide the basis of the preliminary thesis statement.

Remember these characteristics of an argumentative thesis statement:

(a) It is one sentence only.

(b) It makes a claim.

(c) Some people would disagree with the claim.

(d) Its main clause expresses the claim.

(e) Frequently, a subordinate part of the thesis statement expresses a contrasting viewpoint (for example, in a subordinate clause beginning with "although").

THESIS STATEMENT FOR A REPORT RESEARCH PAPER

To arrive at a thesis statement for a report, simply ask yourself: "Which area of information do I want to focus on and describe?" Again, your answer will be the basis of your thesis statement. The more general the statement, the longer will be the report; the more specific and narrowed, the shorter it will be. For a one-semester report assignment, you should have a very narrow topic.

The thesis statement of a report has the following qualities:

(a) It is one sentence only.

(b) Its main clause expresses the main topic of the report.

ARGUMENT OR REPORT?

Sometimes it is difficult to establish whether a thesis statement is an argumentative one or a report thesis. Your decision will often depend on the context of the statement. For example, many years ago people were not sure if air pollution was a cause of ill health, and so, at that time, the thesis statement "Air pollution is linked to ill health" would have been an excellent argumentative one. Nowadays, however, the statement would be suitable for a report, not an argument, because the link between air pollution and ill health has been so well proven that no one would try to deny it.

Another way in which a thesis can be affected is by changing the social context in which it is applied. For instance, the thesis statement "Women teachers should be paid as much as men" is not a valid argumentative one when applied to countries where there is no such discrimination. Yet in some other countries men and women teachers are not paid the same for doing the same work, and so the same statement would, in reference to them, be a good argumentative thesis statement.

Examples

Here are some examples of **argumentative thesis statements**:

Example ▶ **1.** *Domiciliary treatment of tuberculosis has better results for the patients than isolation treatment within hospitals.* (Ines Dourado) This statement makes it clear that Ines will compare the results of the two ways of treating tuberculosis patients. She will aim to prove her assertion that one of them is better.

Example ▶ **2.** *Coal is the best alternative as a substitute for oil in the near future.* (Maite Terrer) From this thesis statement we can see that Maite will discuss various alternatives to oil as a source of energy. She must prove her claim that coal is the best one.

Example ▶ **3.** *Although many people believe that the realist method of staging is the best way to interpret a play, it is a limited form because art must recreate, not copy, life.* (Deolindo Checcucci) To arrive at this thesis statement, Deolindo asked himself, "As an art form, what is the realist method of staging plays really like?" His answer was that it was limited, but he knew from his reading that many people believed it to be the best way to interpret a play. Therefore, his argument is given in the main clause ("it is a limited form") and the opposite view is given in a subordinate clause ("Although many people believe that the realist method of staging is the best way to interpret a play . . ."). He has also added, in another subordinate clause, his reason for making the claim (" . . . because art must recreate, not copy, life").

Example 4. *Although smokers and cigarette companies do not like to believe it, smoking is a clear cause of cancer.* (Jehad Asfoura)
Jehad's question was, "How strong is the connection between smoking and cancer?" He realized that some people (usually smokers, tobacco growers, and owners of cigarette companies) said there was no connection, others said there was a slight connection, and still others said there was a strong connection. From his reading he was convinced that smoking is a clear cause of cancer, and so his belief is given in the main clause of his thesis statement.

Here are two examples of **report thesis statements**, the ones that do not make a claim that must be proved:

Example 5. *Taking good photographs not only depends on having a camera, but also on combining the few fundamentals of color, light, weather conditions, techniques, and accessories.* (Anavat Khavpatumthip)
This thesis statement tells the reader that Anavat's paper will describe the different things that need to be considered in taking photographs. There is no assertion here that needs argumentative proof because the paper will be reporting what is generally accepted by photographers. There is nothing controversial in the statement, nothing that an experienced photographer could disagree with.

Example 6. *Good nutrition, balanced diet, and exercise are important for good health.* (Teresa Alvarez)
Teresa's report thesis statement expresses an idea that is accepted by experts and by others who study human health. It is suitable for a report because it does not make a claim that must be proved. Her paper will go on to give specific information about what exactly good nutrition, balanced diet, and exercise involve, and why they are important.

Exercises: Thesis Statements

Exercise 1

Label each of the following according to the type of topic or thesis statement that it expresses. The first two have been done for you. Be prepared to give reasons for your choices. Use the following abbreviations:

general topic—GT

narrowed topic—NT

argumentative thesis statement—ATS

report thesis statement—RTS

Start by deciding if the sentence is grammatically complete (that is, whether it has a full verb and is an independent clause). If it is a complete sentence, then it will be either a report thesis statement (RTS) or an argumentative thesis statement (ATS). If it is not a complete sentence, then it states either a general topic (GT) or a narrowed topic (NT).

1. _ATS_ Transportation of crude oil in ships is no longer worth the cost.

2. _NT_ Methods of moving crude oil over land from one part of the world to another.

3. _____ Pipelines are more effective than ships for the transportation of crude oil.

4. _____ Ships as transportation.

5. _____ The primary cause of the French Revolution.

6. _____ The French Revolution is the most important event in the history of political systems.

7. _____ Although there are difficulties in learning how to use them, certain electronic travel aids, based on ultrasound or laser beams, must be more widely used to help the blind to become more mobile and independent.

8. _____ Ways in which electronic travel aids have been used by the blind.

9. _____ There are several ways in which electronic travel aids have been used by people who are blind.

10. _____ Researchers have proposed new ways of helping the blind to move around by means of new electronic aids.

11. _____ Radio programs are an important form of entertainment for many people.

12. _____ In spite of the fact that freedom of expression is very important, television should be subject to strict censorship in order to
protect viewers from bad influences.

13. _____ Censorship of television programs is a very bad thing because it denies full freedom of expression.

14. _____ The use of television in education.

15. _____ Television is useful in the medical training of first year nursing students.

16. _____ Education should be conducted by television and computers,
which are more effective than most teachers.

17. _____ The humanity, flexibility, and up-to-date information of good
teachers cannot be replaced by computers, no matter how sophisti-
cated the electronic technology becomes.

18. _____ Running and swimming are forms of exercise.

19. _____ Jogging is better exercise than speed walking.

20. _____ As a form of exercise, skiing gives results that are different
from and superior to those of long distance running.

Exercise 2

The following thesis statements are from student research papers. For
each statement, decide if the thesis statement is for an argumentative
paper or for a report. Give a reason for your answer.

(a) The property tax of the United States is effective and a major source
of income on the local government level, but it will have a reduced
role in the future. (Songsan Udomsilp)

(b) When people retire they have to resolve economic problems, search
for new activities, and develop new social roles. (Maria Luisa Mo-
rales)

(c) Although many people think that mathematics is closest to physics, astronomy, chemistry, and other sciences, some aspects of musical structure and form are akin to mathematical structures and form. (Kanyanit Luengransun)

(d) Nuclear power technology has taken important steps since the early 1970s and, as a result, a new major source of energy has been developed. (Mostefa Ouki)

(e) The primary cause of murine muscular dystrophy may be demyelination of nerve fibers. (Maria Moschella)

(f) Establishing a management information system will help the decision-making unit in an organization solve the problems of management. (Yee-Shioung Lin)

Exercise 3

For each of the thesis statements in Exercise 2, discuss what points should be covered in the body of the paper to ensure a good fit between the paper's content and its thesis statement.

Exercise 4

For three of the following topics, create both an argumentative thesis statement and a report thesis statement.

(a) College education

(b) Violence in TV and movies

(c) Electronic mail

(d) Discipline of children

(e) Capital punishment

(f) Democracy

(g) Growing up

(h) Cultural adjustment

(i) The Internet

(j) Nationalism and violence

Unit 8
Preliminary Outline

Preliminary Outline

Prepare an outline of your research paper. Use numbering and indentation to show the different degrees of importance of the headings and subheadings. Write your preliminary thesis statement before the outline. Hand in the outline to your instructor.

The purpose of outlining is to help you organize your ideas and information and also to generate new ideas. Writing ideas down is a way not only of recording those ideas you have already thought out, but also of encouraging other ideas and new ways of considering them. It helps you see new connections between familiar things. As with note-taking, you can use the writing of a series of outlines as a way of exploring and shaping ideas and not just as a mechanical way of noting what is already formed in your mind.

Although the assignment for this unit requires you to write a formal outline with numbering and indentation, such outlines do not necessarily suit all writers or all writing tasks. Some writers feel that writing a formal outline interferes with their drafting process. Some write formal outlines only for expository, academic writing. You may find that a less formal or different type of outline will suit your own composing process better. For example, some writers just list all the points to be mentioned, and some use a "tree" diagram or "wheel and spokes" diagram to show the relationships between main ideas and supporting ideas.

The statements of your formal outline may all be written in full sentences, or all in phrases or single words, or as some combination of these. It is often very helpful to use full sentences for major points, while using phrases or words for the less important ones.

The ideas expressed in major headings are always more general than those of subheadings, which refer to more specific, more detailed aspects of the major headings.

Finally, note that the outline required for this unit is "preliminary" because it is always the case that writers change their outlines as they discover new information and find better ways to organize it.

Examples: Preliminary Thesis Statement and Outline

Notice that the first example has three levels of numbering and indentation. The other two examples have two levels. The number of levels depends upon the complexity of the material and the degree to which it has been organized by the writer.

The type of numbering system does not matter, but it should be consistent within any one outline. It is not necessary to include the headings "introduction" and "conclusion" because the first main point will automatically be considered the introduction and the last main point will be considered the conclusion.

Example **1.** (Jose Mugica)
Preliminary thesis statement:
Predominantly agricultural, the Dominican Republic needs specific information to give impetus to its economic development.

Outline:
I. There is no possible agricultural development without specific and updated information.
II. The National Documentation Center for Agriculture must confront the problem.
  A. The status of agricultural information in the Dominican Republic
  B. The services of the National Documentation Center for Agriculture
    1. Exchange documents
    2. Photocopies
    3. Loan of documents
    4. Daily press bulletin

     5. Technical consultations

     6. General summaries

III. The main purposes of the National Documentation Center for Agriculture must be fulfilled to improve the Inter-American Agricultural System.

  A. Providing specific information

  B. Distributing the information

  C. Coordinating the National Network for Agriculture

IV. It is necessary to solve the problem found in the execution of the activities.

  A. The role of the Secretary of Agriculture

       Timely distribution of resources

  B. International technical assistance

     1. Role of the International Institute for Agricultural Cooperation (AICA)

     2. Role of the Food and Agricultural Organization (FAO)

Example ▶ **2.** (Juan Carrasco)

Preliminary thesis statement:

Man has been developing art for more than forty thousand years because he can overcome his separateness only through the communication and comprehension of his feelings.

Outline:

  I. Artistic language needs to be learned like any other language, and perhaps it is one of the hardest to learn.

    A. What is drawing?

    B. Two main categories of drawing

    C. The graphic elements

  II. Four factors influence the expressiveness of graphic elements.

    A. The form of perception

    B. The artist's mind

    C. Technical media

    D. Universal symbols

III. Two drawings can be analyzed to illustrate some of the factors previously summarized.

    A. Line

    B. Form

    C. Value and texture

IV. Learning artistic language leads to a changed sensibility and receptive attitude.

Example ▸ **3.** (Synian Hwang)
Preliminary thesis statement:
Statisticians must now consider aspects of the theoretical developments in the sampling theorem under the finite population model.

Outline:
  I. Foundations of survey sampling
      A. Classical finite population model
      B. Current finite population model
 II. An old approach to finite population sampling theory
      A. Basic model
      B. The likelihood function
      C. Best-supported estimates
      D. The role of randomization
III. Sampling theory under certain linear regression models
      A. Basic model
      B. Choice of estimator
      C. Choice of sampling plan
      D. The role of randomization
      E. Some empirical results
 IV. Subjective Bayesian models
      A. Basic model
      B. Exchangeable priors
      C. Results for specific distributions
  V. Future study
      A. Missing data
      B. General model

Unit 9
Plagiarism

Plagiarism, defined in dictionaries as *stealing and using the ideas or writings of another person as one's own,* must be clearly understood and carefully avoided by anyone writing a research paper. Unlike many other types of composition, in which the ideas come directly from the writer and are therefore the "property of" or "owned by" that writer, a research paper necessarily contains great amounts of information and many ideas from the work of others. Also, a research paper may include the words or language used by others.

These two elements—ideas and language—must be acknowledged in citations when they are derived from other writers. Examine published, scholarly articles in your field, and you will see that they have many citations. Notice also that, in addition to the function of acknowledging sources, citations have another important role: they indicate how the ideas in the paper are related to the work of others who have written about the subject.

Consequently, it is important that, when you are taking notes from sources, you should indicate **very carefully** in your own notes the following three types of use:

1. *Language,* including short phrases, *copied directly* from the source. Use quotation marks to show this and note the author's name, the publication, and the page numbers.

2. *Language* which is *all your own* (paraphrase), but which *expresses the author's ideas.* For these notes, you do not need quotation marks, but you must again note the author's name, the publication, and the page numbers.

3. *Words* and *ideas* that are *entirely your own.* These are indicated by the absence of quotation marks and source information.

If you do not make these different kinds of use clear in your note-taking, you will find yourself in a difficult situation when using the notes to write your paper because it will be impossible to remember exactly which words are of which type. You may then end up with *unintentional* plagiarism in your final draft.

A complicating factor for some students whose first language is not English is the fact that different cultures may have different attitudes toward using others' words and ideas without acknowledgment. In some cultures, it may be acceptable because everyone agrees that the words of the original could not be improved. In others, it may be acceptable because the source is considered an authority whose words and ideas are common property as soon as they are published. In yet others it might be regarded as disrespectful and even deceitful to change the words of an original source so they are no longer recognizable.

So, for practical purposes, students from some non–English-speaking backgrounds may have to learn to work with a different set of values when using the language and ideas of others in a research paper. These values are based on the idea that it is a serious crime to plagiarize, so serious that in some cases it has led to students being expelled from schools. The whole issue of plagiarism is a very difficult one to deal with initially, but there are some specific and practical writing guidelines you can learn to follow that will ensure that you do not even unintentionally plagiarize.

GUIDELINES

Follow the four guidelines given here, and you will never be guilty of plagiarism. The first three guidelines refer to using another writer's words. The fourth refers to using someone else's ideas.

Plagiarism of Language

1. Use your own words and sentence structures when writing your paper, even when you are writing about the ideas of others.

2. When paraphrasing (putting someone else's ideas into your own words), avoid using *any* words from the original unless they are essential technical terms.

3. If you use any of the original words from a source, you must acknowledge them by enclosing them in quotation marks. It is still

regarded as plagiarism if, without quotation marks, you use some of the original words and phrases from a sentence and change others. Also, it is still regarded as plagiarism if you keep the sentence structure of the original and change all the words to synonyms.

Plagiarism of ideas

4. Acknowledge all ideas taken from other writers, either in a footnote or as part of the sentence describing the ideas. This applies to any ideas or theories that specialists in the field can recognize as belonging to a specific person. It does not apply to ideas and information that are common knowledge in the field. This is the most difficult area in which to judge whether something is plagiarized because, over the years, ideas that originate with an individual become so generally accepted that their origin is forgotten, and the idea becomes part of the body of knowledge that is central to the subject area and that appears in school textbooks.

In order to get a better understanding of these guidelines, study the following examples of how a text might be used.

Original text:
The second problem would have guaranteed the failure of the new math even if the first problem had not existed. The overwhelming majority of elementary-school teachers have had inadequate training in mathematics, and thus did not understand what they were expected to teach. A program that attempts to transmit knowledge not possessed by the teacher is doomed to fail. As this fact became clear to curriculum directors and textbook publishers across the country, they compounded their error by attempting to make the new math teacher-proof. This involved developing self-explanatory materials and mechanical, repetitive techniques which were based on underlying mathematical principles. Unfortunately, the new techniques were far more complicated than the old ones had been, the teachers still didn't understand what was going on, and an entire generation did not learn how to compute. (Copperman, P. (1980). *The literacy hoax*. New York: Morrow Quill Paperbacks, p. 65)

Possible uses of this text:

Example 1.
PLAGIARISM (This should be in quotation marks.)
> A program that attempts to transmit knowledge not possessed by the teacher is doomed to fail!

NOT PLAGIARISM (The quotation marks and citation make this an acceptable use of the original.)
> "A program that attempts to transmit knowledge not possessed by the teacher is doomed to fail" (Copperman, 1980, p. 65).

Example 2.
PLAGIARISM (This is patchwork plagiarism; a few words are paraphrased but most are from the original, and the sentence structure is also from the original.)
> A course that attempts to transmit knowledge not possessed by the teacher will never succeed.

NOT PLAGIARISM (The quotation marks around words from the original, and the changed sentence structure for words that are not quoted, make this acceptable.)
> Success is impossible for a course "that attempts to transmit knowledge not possessed by the teacher."

Example 3.
PLAGIARISM (This is plagiarism because the original sentence structure has been kept, even though the writer has used synonyms to replace most words.)
> A course that tries to convey understanding not held by the teacher is fated to be unsuccessful.

NOT PLAGIARISM (This is acceptable because it is a full paraphrase, with original words and sentence structure changed, of an idea that is common knowledge in the field of education.)
> If the instructor does not have the knowledge that the student is meant to learn from a course, then the course will never succeed.

Example 4.

PLAGIARISM (Even though this is a full paraphrase, it is plagiarism of the author's idea from the first sentence of the extract because the idea is not common knowledge in the field of math education.)

> Without the first problem, the second one would still have been enough to stop the new math from working.

NOT PLAGIARISM (This is acceptable because it is a full paraphrase and the author's own idea has been clearly attributed to him.)

> Copperman (1980, p. 65) claims that, without the first problem, the second one would still have been enough to stop the new math from working.

NOT PLAGIARISM (This is acceptable because it is a full paraphrase and the author's own idea has been clearly attributed to him.)

> Without the first problem, the second one would still have been enough to stop the new math from working (Copperman, 1980, p. 65).

Exercise

Plagiarism of Language

(Plagiarism of ideas, which must be judged by an expert in the field, is not included in this exercise.)

The extract below is followed by some possible uses that could be made of it. For each use, say whether or not it is plagiarism. Give a reason for your decision.

Original text:

> An even better case can be made that the new English curriculum has directly caused a deterioration in the writing skills of American students. Writing instruction in the early 1960's tended to be rather mechanical. Teachers focused on such aspects of the writing art as grammar, punctuation, syntax, and spelling. This type of instruction was fiercely criticized in the late 1960's as stifling creativity and fostering an imitative kind of writing. In my opinion, some of the criticism was well-founded, especially for bright students, but as usual the baby went out with the bath water. (Copperman, P. (1980). *The literacy hoax*. New York: Morrow Quill Paperbacks, p. 100)

Possible uses of the original text:

1. "...the new English curriculum has directly caused a deterioration in the writing skills of American students."

    Plagiarism ___   Not plagiarism ___

2. Teachers focused on such aspects of the writing art as grammar, punctuation, syntax, and spelling.

    Plagiarism ___   Not plagiarism ___

3. Instructors concentrated on such parts of the skill of written composition as "grammar, punctuation, syntax, and spelling."

    Plagiarism ___   Not plagiarism ___

4. A mechanical approach dominated the teaching of composition in the first years of the 1960's.

    Plagiarism ___   Not plagiarism ___

5. Copperman (1980, p. 100) asserts that there was validity in some of the attacks on early 1960's writing instruction and that what was good was thrown out with what was bad: "...the baby went out with the bath water."

    Plagiarism ___   Not plagiarism ___

6. This type of instruction was fiercely criticized in the late 1960's as stifling creativity and fostering an imitative kind of writing.

    Plagiarism ___   Not plagiarism ___

7. During the later years of the 1960's, two strong criticisms were made of such teaching of writing: first, that the students could not be creative, and, second, that the writing that was encouraged was only copied models.

    Plagiarism ___   Not plagiarism ___

8. One view (Copperman, 1980, p. 100) is that, although there was good evidence to support some of the critical judgments, the effective aspects of instruction were given up together with the ineffective.

    Plagiarism ___   Not plagiarism ___

Unit 10
Taking Notes

Taking Notes

Over a period of a few weeks, take notes from various sources for your paper. From your set of notes, select some to hand in to your instructor. Each note must indicate the source and page numbers.

The notes that you hand in must include two examples of each of the following:

1. Summaries of two kinds:
   (a) in your own words (paraphrase)
   (b) using direct quotation (indicated by quotation marks)

2. Nonsummarized notes of two kinds:
   (a) in your own words (paraphrase)
   (b) direct quotation (indicated by quotation marks)

3. Notes with abbreviations for some or many words

Taking notes well is an important skill in the process of research paper writing. It has three purposes:

(a) To record information so that you do not forget it

(b) To help you to understand and organize the ideas and information that you get from your reading

(c) To give you a chance to develop and record your own ideas about your topic, ideas that are stimulated by what you read and by the act of writing

TECHNIQUES FOR TAKING NOTES

Notes may be taken on sheets of paper or on file cards.

You will save yourself from confusing your notes later in the writing process if you make sure now that each note has a clear indication of which source it comes from. Each must also show the exact page numbers that are the origin of the note.

The source may be indicated by using the name of the author. For example, write "Johnson" (at the beginning of the note or in a corner) for a book or article by Daniel P. Johnson. Another way is to give each one of your preliminary bibliography entries a code number or letter; then use that number or letter on your notes. For example, the book or article by Daniel P. Johnson may have a code letter *J*, in which case each note card from that source will have "J" written in one of the corners. You can no doubt invent other ways of keeping track of sources—the important thing is to note all sources.

Another technique you can use to help you plan your ideas later, when you are trying out different ways of organizing the information, is to give each note a brief heading related to the content. One or two words or a short phrase indicating which aspect of your subject is dealt with in each note is enough. Write this heading at the beginning or in one of the corners (and place it in parentheses).

The most important thing to remember when taking notes is that you must put quotation marks around all words that are not your own (except for technical terms that are common in the subject area). This is because in your paper you must show clearly which words and ideas are from sources you have read. If you do not show this clearly, you will be guilty of plagiarism.

TYPES OF NOTES

Notes are of different kinds: Some are *direct quotations* of the author's words. Others are *paraphrase,* giving the same information as the source but entirely in the words of the researcher. Others are *summaries* of the main ideas, in either the author's or the researcher's words. Many notes are *combinations* of these types.

The most common type is a combination of paraphrase and summary, using the writer's own word or phrase abbreviations and including some direct quotation.

When taking notes you should not rely upon too many direct quotations, because they will form only a small part of your final paper (perhaps ten percent or less). Sometimes, however, students feel that they should copy down as much as possible (or even photocopy a lot), and they tell themselves that "later" they will try to understand what they have noted (or photocopied). This is a very poor strategy to use, because it leads to a situation in which there is too much to digest at the last minute.

Remember that a research paper is a long-term, not a short-term, project. You should therefore use the note-taking period very carefully; this is the time when you develop a real understanding of your topic. It is also the time when you begin to realize what changes must be made in your preliminary thesis statement and outline, and it is the time when you discover which items to drop from your preliminary bibliography and which new ones to add.

CHANGING IDEAS AND GETTING NEW IDEAS WHILE TAKING NOTES

Often writers of research papers get very anxious about the project during the note-taking phase because their ideas and plans keep developing and changing and because they find more references to things that they should read. This is in fact no cause for concern. It is a natural part of writing a long composition that uses sources of information other than your own experience.

The aim of your research is to put yourself in a position in which your knowledge and ideas develop and change. You are researching because you want to move from knowing a little about your topic to being an expert on it. So make full use of the activity of note-taking as an important way of developing good understanding of your subject. Writing down facts and ideas stimulates thinking about the topic and about the connections between different aspects of it. Expect your ideas to change and develop during note-taking.

Examples

Look at the following examples of different types of notes. They were written by Maite Terrer for her paper on coal as an energy source and by Jehad Asfoura for his paper on the link between smoking and cancer. Maite used letter codes (*D, C, E,* etc.) to indicate the sources of her notes. Jehad used authors' names to keep track of sources.

Example 1. Direct quotation and summary with abbreviations (the most common type of note-taking)

(cost/demand) D p. 56

"Nevertheless, higher cost marginal coal mines will only be developed if there is sufficient demand for coal at prices that will cover costs, and there will only be sufficient demand for coal if coal is a competitive source of energy."
    Oil will be more expensive in future, so products fr. coal conv. will compete. Diff betw coal and oil prices will be lg. enough to allow for high cost of coal conv. and prodn of compet prods. Rise in oil price cd affect demand for coal by increasing prodn and transp costs. But compet between coal prods and those fr oil may limit incr. of oil prices in future.

Example ▶ 2. Summary with abbreviations

(coal-based technology) C 13-19

Impt. to consider tech based on coal because of c's avail. and the possib it cd. subst. for oil as an energy resource.

There are technols. capable of using c. to obt. products to subst. for natural oil and gas, e.g. c. gasification gives several kinds of products, such as low or medium BTH gas, wh. can be transformed by other processes into other gaseous & liquid fuels.

Example ▶ 3. Summary, with abbreviations, and some direct quotations

---

(expanded use) E microfilm 1-10

It is nec. to incr. the prodn. of coal to "provide a transition" (p. 1) betw. oil and other energy sources. "Because of its abundance and versatility (it can be converted to coke, synthetic gases, liquids and chemical feedstocks) coal is one of the only alternatives to oil, natural gas and nuclear power in the near term that can rapidly increase to meet demands (p. 3).
At pres. coal supplies more than 1/4 world energy, but will have to supp. betw. 1/2 and 2/3 of the additional energy needed by the world dur. next 20 yrs. To do so coal prod. must incr. 2 1/2 to 3 x and world trade in steam coal must grow 10 to 15 X. Study's concl. is simple: "Without such a coal expansion the world economic outlook is bleak." (p. 10)

Example 4. Summary, with abbreviations, and two short direct quotations

---

(coal-usage advantages) D 65

- c. mining industries - employment increase. (also in related transportn. industries)
- countries w. no c will save by purchase of coal inst. of oil, for gen. of elec. & other industrial applics.
- subst. by coal will allow the "diversification of energy supplies" & reductions in oil-import. dependency
- utilizn. of c may incr. the dev. of new technols. wh. cd. allow subst. of oil by gas & liquid fuels from coal and "higher utilization of the infrastructure for liquid and gas fuel distribution."

Example 5. Summary with abbreviations

(coal production costs) D (1) 55-56

Usually t. coal industry has a steady level of cost.
Future: prices will rise, but less rise than that of oil prices.
Cost of mining coal cd. be "moderated by increases in labor productivity" resulting from:

i) gradual intro. of new mining technologies

ii) opening of new, more productive c. mines

iii) expected shift to large-scale surface mining in major c. prod countries.

Coal prodn. costs will rise if there is little devpt. of productive mines. This will affect c's competitiveness with alternative energy supplies.

Example ► **6.** Paraphrase and summary

(PIPE vs. CIGAR)   Rogers p. 43

The incidence of cancer is less among the smokers of pipes or cigars if we compare them with the cigarette smokers. This fact is related to the filtering qualities of the pipe or the cigar, and the lower consumption of tobacco among the pipe or cigar smokers.

   The pipe tar is a reason for cancer lesions which cause the death of mice in 2-3 weeks.

Example ► **7.** Mainly direct quotation

(TYPES OF CANCER) Culvihill p. 23

The kinds of cancer which are caused by cigarette smoke and their sites.
   "lung - epidermoid
   mouth and throat - squamous cell
   larynx - squamous cell
   esophagus - squamous cell
   bladder - transitional"

Example ► **8.** All direct quotation

(EFFECTS OF GIVING UP) Franks et al. p. 85

"The cessation of smoking reverses the early pathological changes; as a result, it prevents people from getting cancer, but it cannot reverse the very old changes. They take several years to extinguish."

Example ▶ **9.** Mainly paraphrase, with some direct quotation

---

(TOXINS IN SMOKE) Lee & Aloysius p. 85

Numerous toxins in cigarette smoke interfere with the influences of smoking in the organism: Acrolein, Nitrogen dioxide, Hydrogen cyanide, Carbon monoxide, but the most important toxin is Polycyclihydrocarbon "whose possible carcinogenicity has been receiving increasing attention."

Example ▶ **10.** All direct quotation

(RISK STATISTICS) Rogers p. 309

"No. of cigarettes	No. of cases	No. of controls	Ratio	Relative Risk
0	3	14	0.21	1.00
1-9	1	4	0.25	1.77
10-19	8	16	0.50	2.33
20-29	24	14	1.71	0.00
30-39	9	4	2.25	10.50
40	9	2	4.50	21.00

It demonstrates the relationship of smoking to case-control status. There is a direct increase of risk with amount smoked, using the non-smoker as the reference point (relative risk = 1)"

Example **11.** Paraphrase with no summarizing

(SMOKERS/NON-SMOKERS) Franks et al. p.7
(HEAVY/LIGHT SMOKERS)

It has been proved since 1952 in research described to the
American Cancer Society by Dr. Cyder Hammond that
cigarette smokers die from cancer and heart diseases
before non-smokers in the forty to seventy age range.
There are many known facts about cancer and smoking.
Light and heavy smoking is associated with an increase of
the death rate, especially from the organs in which cancer
appears, but heavy smoking decides the death rate, and
also there is no difference between the rural or the sub-
rural areas in this problem.

Unit 11
Revised Thesis Statement

RP Assignment

Revising Your Thesis Statement

Revise your thesis statement on the basis of the new ideas and insights you have developed during note-taking. Write down the following:

(a) Your revised thesis statement (one sentence)

(b) Your preliminary thesis statement (one sentence)

Add a brief explanation of why you have changed your thesis statement in this way.

If you do not want to change your preliminary thesis statement, write it down in its original form and add next to it: NO CHANGE.

Your preliminary thesis statement is not likely to remain unchanged. It was formulated at a stage in the research paper process when you knew much less than you do now. On the basis of preliminary reading, you previously came up with a thesis statement that you felt would possibly express your controlling idea. It was a guide and focus for your reading. Now that you have done more, or most, of your reading and note-taking, you are in a position to know how you will have to change your preliminary thesis statement.

After reading and note-taking, many researchers find that they can narrow down their thesis statements more than they originally thought. Others refine or change the thesis statement in small ways. In the case of argumentative research papers, some writers realize that their thesis statement should be making a different claim (occasionally *very* different) from the one that they started with.

Such changes and developments are to be welcomed. They are part of the normal flow of research; they are not indications of confusion and inconsistency. The purpose of your reading and research is to find out new information and ideas. So you must expect to modify and change your ideas, even possibly the main idea, as you move from knowing little to knowing a lot.

During the process of writing an argumentative paper, the thesis statement is very likely to be changed. The thesis statement of a report research paper, in contrast to that of an argumentative one, is less likely to be changed in any major ways, but will probably be narrowed down more.

Unit 12
Revised Outline

RP Assignment

Revising Your Outline

Revise your outline on the basis of the new ideas you have developed during your note-taking. Again use numbers, letters, and indentation to show the relative importance and relationship of ideas. Hand in your preliminary outline together with the revised one.

The outline that you prepare at this stage should be more detailed than the preliminary one. However, it still remains a guide. It is not something that restricts you; do not feel trapped by your outline.

After all the reading and note-taking that you have now done, there should be a clearer framework of thoughts in your mind for the overall structure of the paper—that is, for how the main sections will connect with your thesis statement and how the subsections will tie in with the main sections. The numbers, letters, and indentation of the outline are indications of how your ideas relate to each other. You should experiment or "play with" parts of the outline—trying them in different orders—in order to find different, perhaps better, ways to sort things out.

Writing an outline in this way and revising it helps you to discover new ways of organizing your information. It is not the same thing as turning over in your mind the different possibilities without ever writing them down. Seeing ideas in written form on paper gives you a different kind of opportunity to change them and reorganize them. Revising the outline stimulates new ideas and new ways of looking at your material.

Whatever outline you produce now, remember that it may still be changed. It may indeed change several more times because the process of producing your research paper is an ongoing one, with potential for change and improvement at all stages before the final draft.

Unit 13

Starting the Preliminary Draft

Many writers of research papers worry most of all at this point in the activity because this is when they must begin to produce large amounts of written text. However, the worry occurs only because they misunderstand what they have to do. They do *not* have to produce perfect sentences, one after another, building up into good paragraphs that become a good final product, all in the first rough draft. Skilled and experienced writers do not normally work this way.

DRAFTING PROCESS

The normal drafting process that you should learn to feel comfortable with, by practicing it now, is as follows:

1. Select the part of the paper that you want to work on.

2. Carefully read your notes relevant to that section. Read the notes more than once, so that you get a very good understanding of the ideas and the points you want to make.

3. Begin to write what you think might *possibly* be a relevant set of ideas. Do not imagine that you must write very logically and correctly at this point. Have only one aim as you start on the draft—to let the ideas come out onto the page. No one except you will see what you are writing now, so do not let your thoughts about correctness and coherence control the process at this time.

4. When you run out of ideas, go back to your notes and read them again. Use them to stimulate a fresh flow of thoughts. Write these down as they come to you.

5. When you run out of ideas again, and your notes give you no further help—which is the natural state of affairs, even for professional writers—you can begin to work on some other part of your paper or re-read what you have written so far. If this does not help, you need a break from the work!

6. If you choose to go over what you have written so far, you can now begin to change the order of ideas, omit some ideas, or add new ones; you can now cross out, add to, or change any of the words, phrases, clauses, or sentences. Or, as some writers do, you may just reread what you have drafted as a preliminary to writing another rough draft.

7. You may decide to produce several rough drafts for this assignment. Or you may produce only one. Whatever the case, it is only while writing the final version that you will hand in to your instructor that you should be concerned with details of grammar, spelling, and punctuation.

Remember: the seemingly messy and disorganized stages of writing drafts are an ordinary and perfectly natural part of composing. Not only are they natural and ordinary, they are actually essential. Before you can begin to organize a mixed bag of ideas, you must spread them out before yourself—get them down on paper somehow. Often, you will not have an exact idea of the contents of the bag before you spread the ideas out; and when you first look at what comes out, you may think that it is all too chaotic and disorganized to make sense of. However, if you study it long enough, you will begin to make sense of it. You will begin to see patterns—relationships between the ideas and facts. Discovering these connections through a discovery draft is part of the writing process.

The process described here is the same for all writers, but ESL students often feel helpless and frustrated at the thought of a research paper to be written, and they imagine that their difficulties are all due to language use. In fact, native speakers of English, including experienced writers, very often feel the same way. Writing frequently involves periods of feeling "blank", "dry", or "without ideas." This feeling, which writers quite often suffer from—that they cannot continue, that they have nothing to say—is called writer's block. It is a terrible sensation but it passes! You can help it pass by just taking a break or by working on a different part of the paper.

Finally, remember that a long research paper, just like published books and articles, is the outcome of many drafts and much revising. Your paper will be written in sections and parts over a period of many weeks, and the order in which you work on the parts is not likely to be their order in the final draft. Never expect to write such a paper straight through from beginning to end even if you have excellent notes.

EXAMPLE OF A ROUGH DRAFT

The part of a rough draft shown on page 77 is one of the many drafts written for the explanation of this unit. It is an example of one stage that one writer went through before arriving at a version that could be given to someone else to read. You will go through some similar drafting stages to produce the two pages required for the assignment in this unit and, later, to produce the other parts of your research paper. (*Note:* The two pages to be handed in to your instructor, required as the assignment for this unit, should *not* look like the following rough draft; your two pages must be a revised, neater version of a preliminary rough draft.)

Marking the pages of a printed draft as in this example is not the only way to reorganize the parts of a rough draft. Many writers rearrange the sections of a draft by means of a "cut and paste" method. If they are using a computer, they can cut and paste electronically. If handwriting, they may use scissors to cut up the pages of the draft into segments that are then moved and stuck into their new positions.

as necessary

go back over this and change ∧ the order of ideas, cross out

parts, insert new ~~ideas~~ words, phrases and sentences, ~~and so~~

~~on.~~ Remember that ~~the~~ **a** final draft of good writing has

is seemingly

always <u>first</u> gone through the ∧ messy, apparently disorganized

stage. No one ever produces a ~~polished researc pap~~ good

piece of expository writing without going through the ~~initial~~

~~stages~~ phases of apparent chaos. It is quite ~~distressing~~ to

sometimes   worrying

∧

⌐ PAR

inexperienced ~~writing~~ writers to see that they cannot write

~~excellently~~ perfectly on the very first draft. Sometimes this

even

worry prevents them from ∧ trying to start. Their anxiety is not

necessary. Too much of this type of anxiety is a hinderance

not a help, though a small amount of it, a little adrenalin, is

sometimes thought to be helpful. The books and articles they

to end

see published are all the outcome of much drafting and

Unit 14

Completing the Preliminary Draft

Preliminary Draft

Prepare a complete draft of your research paper, consisting of the following parts:
   Cover page
   Thesis statement and outline
   Text of the paper, consisting of:
      Introduction
      Body (development)
      Conclusion
   Bibliography
Although this will not be the final version of your paper, it should be presented in a neat and clear way.

If you do not follow the APA format and documentation style described in units 16 and 17, then you must submit with your draft one or two photocopied pages from a published example of the style you are following. (Refer to the appendix on p. 140 for a list of style guides.)

The aim of writing this preliminary draft is to make an attempt to draft a whole paper—to bring together all of its parts. The text of the paper (the introduction, body, and conclusion) is what will occupy you most of all at this stage. This is where you draft and redraft sections of the paper. It is where you organize and reorganize words, phrases, clauses, sentences, paragraphs, and larger units. Other than writing the text of your paper, the requirements of this assignment are mechanical. They are concerned with layout and acknowledgments of sources. (Units 16 and 17 give information about and examples of different formats.)

The parts of this assignment are the same as those you will be asked for in the final draft. They are all required here in order to give your instructor an opportunity to help you with all aspects of the paper—from small points of grammar and format to larger issues of overall organization and coherence.

COVER PAGE

A cover page for an academic paper has no purpose other than to give your work an efficient and neat look and to help your instructor (whose desk is probably covered with papers from several courses) keep track of all the papers he or she must deal with. Write the title of your paper in the center of the page. Below that, write your name, your class or course number, the instructor's name, and the date.

TITLE

The title should be a phrase (not a complete sentence) that informs your reader about the content of the paper. It should not be too long, and it should not be so short that it is too vague and general. If you want to, you can add a subtitle after a colon.

THESIS STATEMENT AND OUTLINE

Although your instructor has already seen your preliminary and revised outlines, they are included in this draft because you can revise them again. Also, when reading your paper, your instructor can use your thesis statement and outline as a guide to understanding the intended structure of your paper. Inclusion of these is not, however, a requirement in papers for academic courses. In a paper for publication, an abstract (summary) is often placed at the beginning.

TEXT OF THE PAPER

As stated previously, the text of the paper—introduction, body, and conclusion—is the part that you spend the most time on. This is what most people refer to as "composing a paper"—writing several or many pages of coherent text. In fact, the composing process really started as soon as you were given the task and began your search for a topic. All your thinking about the paper is part of composing it; even before you settle on a definite idea or topic for the paper, you have begun composing.

By now, you have already done a great amount of work toward the paper: narrowing the subject, reading for a preliminary bibliography, preparing preliminary and revised versions of your thesis statement and outline, taking notes, and writing a draft of part of the paper. So do not think of this as the beginning of the "real" task of writing the paper. Writing a paper consists of getting ideas, playing with them, refining them, changing them, reading about the subject, note-taking, drafting a paragraph or two, revising—all of this is part of the process.

As you write this preliminary draft, think of it as a tryout of how a certain set of ideas and sentences will look on the page; imagine that you are playing with ways of putting together all that you know. This is not the final draft, so do not inhibit yourself by believing that it should all come out completely coherent and well polished. It should of course be legible and neat; your instructor cannot help you if the draft is difficult to read.

The draft you hand in may not be the very first one you write. Most writers agree that in writing the first draft they are somehow discovering what they want to say. That is, what comes out in this draft will be something that the writer of the paper may use only as a starting point. It is a way of seeing, all in one place, what is available. And the way it comes out is just one way of organizing it. As the writer looks over the very first draft, other ways of organizing it may occur to him or her; new ideas about the content may come to mind; new refinements of the thesis statement may come about. All this can be included in the later drafts, one of which can be the preliminary draft turned in to the instructor.

In composing the text of the paper, do not let yourself get stuck on any one part—whether the introduction or any other. If you find you are not making progress on one section, move on to another. Research papers are not written in one, single beginning-to-end flow. Work on different parts, using your outline as a guide, to avoid the frustration of feeling that you are at a dead end.

LINKING PARTS OF THE PAPER: TRANSITIONS

When you have written enough on each separate section of the paper to put together a reasonable preliminary draft, give careful thought to joining the parts with good **transitions** (also called connectors, linking elements, or cohesive devices). It is these transitions that enable the reader to follow your train of thought easily.

Between major sections, you will sometimes need a complete, short paragraph whose only function is to provide the transition.

Between paragraphs, you will usually need a transitional sentence or phrase at the end of the first paragraph or the beginning of the next one.

Between sentences, you will often need transitional words or phrases, repetition of key words, or reference words (such as pronouns and demonstratives) to create cohesion.

ORGANIZATION OF IDEAS AND INFORMATION

There are many ways of organizing information in a research paper; the ones you choose will be determined by your purpose. The following are the most common organizational patterns:

Chronological order—time order: first to last or last to first

Spatial arrangement—physical location of parts

Comparison—similarities and differences

Analogy—a comparison emphasizing similarities

Contrast—a comparison emphasizing differences

Increasing importance—from least to most important

Decreasing importance—from most to least important

Decreasing generality—from general to specific

Increasing generality—from specific to general

Development by examples—using examples to support explanations

Cause and effect—what happens, with reasons why it happens

Definition—stating the group to which something belongs and how it is different from other members of the same group

Classification—grouping things together in a logical way

Logical division—an analysis into parts

Very few compositions can use only one of these although, in some cases, one pattern (e.g., comparison) may predominate. Most compositions, especially research papers, make use of a combination of various patterns, and it is usually impossible to make neat separations between them in any one paper.

For most writers, it is not very useful to think too much about the exact patterns that are to be used. Instead, when writing your paper, think of the ideas that are to be conveyed and try to find the words for those ideas. When this is done and you look back over what you have written, you will find that it probably falls quite naturally and without deliberate planning into the appropriate patterns. Occasionally, however, thinking consciously about the rhetorical patterns can help you to clarify what you want to say.

INTEGRATING IDEAS FROM SOURCES

Unlike a personal essay, a research paper makes many references to the writings of others. It is essential that you carefully distinguish in your paper which words, opinions, and ideas are your own and which ones are from sources. Therefore, you need to practice two specific skills for integrating the ideas of other writers into your paper: direct quotation and paraphrase (stating the ideas of others in your own words).

Direct quotation is not difficult. Simply copy the words of the original and show that these are direct quotation. Either use quotation marks (for short quotations) or indent the whole quotation (for quotations of five or more lines).

Paraphrasing requires the grammar and vocabulary skills needed to restate others' ideas without plagiarizing. It also requires that you use a lot of reported (indirect) speech as you state the ideas of others. Some common verbs used in reporting are the following. (Be careful!— they are not all synonyms of each other; use them according to their different shades of meaning.)

state	maintain	imply
say	observe	suggest
remark	emphasize	explain
comment	declare	propose
claim	contend	report
assert	argue	

Some useful common phrases (where X = name(s) of author(s)) are

according to X

in the opinion of X

X expresses the view that

X presents the idea that

as X says

as reported by X

Some examples of useful expressions referring to studies and research are

the study shows that

her research reveals that

their results demonstrate that

this research proves that

INTRODUCTIONS

Write the introduction to your paper last, so that you can make it a guide to the content and structure of the paper. Remember that you will discover things to say or add or change as you write the first drafts, and so it would be a waste of time to prepare a polished introduction first. By not writing the introduction at the very beginning, you will not feel trapped by it, and your paper will develop more easily.

The first part of your introduction should state the general context of your topic, usually with some reference to work done by others. Then you should indicate what your paper will focus on: your thesis statement comes in at this point. In the last part of your introduction, you should help the reader by giving a very brief summary of the main points you will cover. That is, the main points of your outline should be mentioned here in the form of a few consecutive sentences (not in the indented and numbered format of the outline).

BODY (DEVELOPMENT)

The largest single part of the paper is the body, which consists of supporting information or arguments relevant to the main idea expressed in the thesis statement. Whereas, in a short paper, the introduction and conclusion may each be just one paragraph, the body is composed of many paragraphs.

CONCLUSIONS

A good conclusion to a research paper is the logical outcome of all that has been said earlier. Usually, the thesis statement is repeated but not in exactly the same wording. Sometimes certain actions or further research are recommended in a conclusion. And occasionally a research paper ends with an effective quotation. When writing the conclusion to your paper, you should aim not to end too suddenly, too abruptly. So it is useful to restate the main points of your paper in a very summarized form and in different words before restating the controlling idea.

USING QUOTATIONS

Although direct quotations appear in most research papers, they are not usually an important part of them. Some papers make very little use of quotations. Reference to the work of others is central to research papers, but most of the reference is in the form of indirect speech. You should use direct quotations only when they are very relevant, when they express something in a very special or effective way, or when they are good examples of ideas that you will focus on. As a general guideline, try to keep direct quotations at well below ten percent of your whole paper. Your instructor is, after all, interested in how you express yourself and not interested in the words of others.

Take care to weave direct quotations smoothly into the text of your paper by using suitable introductory phrases and expressions. (See unit 16 for examples and formats of long and short quotations.)

KEEPING YOUR READER IN MIND

As you write, you will constantly be making decisions about what to put into the paper and what to leave out. The choice is determined by who will read what you write.

Although you will be handing your paper in to one instructor, you should not think of that individual as the audience or reader of your paper. A research paper is written for an audience that is knowledgeable in the subject. Therefore, you should think of the instructor as being typical of such an audience, but do not try to work out exactly what this individual instructor knows about your topic. Instead, from your reading of books and articles, you will get an understanding of what is common knowledge in the field and what is specialized. Think of your readers as having a good general knowledge of the subject and some specialized knowledge about your narrowed topic. Think of yourself as the expert in the very specific focus of your thesis statement. In this way you will not include information that is well known to your readers, and you will not leave out what is needed for them to follow your discussion. This is especially important in argumentative papers. In writing a report, you can avoid telling your readers what they already know if you emphasize up-to-date ideas and information, for example, from recent journal articles (not from standard textbooks or encyclopedias, which include what the audience should know quite well).

Exercise 1
Linking Parts of the Paper: Transitions

Read the following paragraphs from the body of a paper by Myaw-Ing Shyu. (She wrote about foreign students investing in mutual funds.) Answer the questions. The paragraphs are numbered for ease of reference in this exercise.

Extract from the body of Myaw-Ing's paper

1   The fourth type is income funds. Their purpose is to maximize the shareholders' current return. Income funds may be common stock

funds or balanced funds. Due to the stress on current return, they may increase slightly in net asset value and decrease in price stability (Mead, 1991, pp. 8–16).

2   The fifth and last kind is international funds. "The purpose of the international funds is to invest the cash provided by their shareholders in securities of firms that are incorporated under the law of nations other than the United States" (Mead, 1991, pp. 16). International funds usually invest mostly in other countries' bonds and stocks.

3   After understanding these different types of funds, investors may still not know what is the best choice of fund. Therefore, some criteria for choosing are suggested below. There are five key issues that investors must consider before they decide to buy mutual funds: risk, cost, time-frame, performance history, and objective.

4   With regard to risk, investors should understand their own attitude toward risk. They should decide how much risk they are willing to take: high, medium, or low risk or some of each. Does an investor prefer regular dividends or growth stocks which increase in value but do not pay dividends (Govoni, 1992, p. 39)? Investors had better not to try to take more risk than they can handle; or they will react badly, selling at the bottom after buying at the top (Baldwin, 1992, p. 86). Though high risk usually means high return, it also means possible high loss. Thus, if an investor is a conservative person, it is better for him/her, not to try such mutual funds. On the other hand, if he/she is a risk-taking person, these may be good alternatives. Because investors are anxious to find ways to do better than low interest rates, most mutual fund advertisements claim high returns at low risk. Investors should not only know about each fund's high returns, but also its losses in the past (Hulbert, 1992, p. 225). Investors must keep in mind that the higher the yield is, the higher the risk (Battle, 1996, p. 57).

5   Cost is also one of the issues investors have to think over because there are many kinds of fund fees: the up front fee, management charge, extra costs, etc. Sometimes these fees cost a lot (Battle, 1996, p. 56). For U.S. funds, the total should not be too much more than 1%; for a foreign fund, 2% is par (Baldwin, 1992, pp. 86–87). Such transaction costs can offset fund yield. Therefore, investors had better avoid buying a fund only for a short term.

6   In addition to risk and cost, time-frame is a factor to consider. Time-frame means how long an investor will own the funds. Some

investors can predict that they will need these monies one year later. They will use the time-frame to think about what kinds of funds are suitable for them to keep for one year, while aiming for low cost and high yield. How long will the money be invested in funds? The term will influence what kind of funds investors should select (Govoni, 1992, p. 39).

7   Performance is the most popular issue that investors use to evaluate a fund. However, past performance is no guarantee of future results. It is not wise for investors to trust in the past performance completely, but combine it with other facts to evaluate the fund (Baldwin, 1992, p. 87). Some funds that have grown slowly may have big advances when investment conditions change. Investors should find figures such as annual net asset values, individual share price, and dividend distributions, going back for as much as ten years (Battle, 1986, p. 57). There is no uniform method for computing the investment yield to compare the performance of funds.

8   Besides the above issues, investors should decide on their investment goals. What is their objective? Every investor has his/her own objective. It may be current income, maximum capital, long-term growth, tax-free income, safety of principal, receiving dividends regularly, or combinations of these (Battle, 1986, p. 87; Govoni, 1992, p. 39). The goal will influence investors' choices.

9   These five issues are important for all investors to consider before they decide to buy mutual funds. These issues are not independent. They may influence each other and should be combined with each other. In order to have the best result, investors, including foreign students, had better not ignore any one of them.

10   Considering the kinds of funds and the criteria for choosing them, how should foreign students go into mutual fund investing? What should they notice? What is the best buy for them?

(a) Which paragraphs are transitional?

(b) In paragraphs 1 and 2, which sentences are transitional?

(c) In paragraph 6, which sentence is transitional?

(d) In the first sentence of paragraph 3, which phrase makes a transition by referring back to earlier information? In the last sentence of the same paragraph, which phrases refer to information that will be discussed in the next part of the paper?

(e) In paragraph 4 (line 9), what is the meaning of the transition "thus"? In the same paragraph (lines 10–11) what is the meaning of the transition "on the other hand"?

(f) In paragraph 7 (line 2), what is the meaning of the transition "however"?

(g) In paragraph 8 (line 1), what is the meaning of the transitional phrase "besides the above"?

(h) In paragraphs 4–8, five issues are discussed. Which phrases in paragraphs 3 and 9 introduce and refer back to the issues?

(i) After reading the questions in paragraph 10, what topics do you expect will be discussed in the following paragraphs?

Exercise 2

Integrating Ideas from Sources: Paraphrasing and Reporting

Read the following paragraphs, which are extracted from a research paper by Mario Vespa. (His subject was the origin of computers.) Then do the exercise.

Two paragraphs from Mario's paper

Let us go back through time until a few thousand years B.C. when people used to show their fingers while they were referring to the number of persons in their families or to animals that they had hunted. Thus, there was a natural pause when they arrived at five, and a longer one when they arrived at ten because they had only ten fingers. This fact was the beginning of considering ten as a counting basis. If our hands had eight fingers, certainly the basis of counting would have been eight instead of ten. Thinking about mathematical concepts, the number twelve would have been better than ten since it is divisible by two, three, four, and six, but using our hands to count, twelve is a very hard unit to handle. However, the activities of people became more and more complex very quickly, and their ten units grew to twenty when they used their fingers and toes. Nevertheless, these twenty units were not enough to handle their world.

Next, a giant step in counting appeared when people started to group rough stones at first, and pebbles later, to represent members of their tribe or enemies whose number was more than twenty. In some agricultural tribes, they put pebbles in front of the granary to show the total amount of grain stored in it. As they added grain to the granary, they added pebbles to the set. On the other hand, when grains were consumed, they took pebbles away. This was the very beginning of the abacus, the first real counting machine.

(a) In your own words, write three separate sentences reporting ideas from Mario's paragraphs. Use the writer's last name when you report the ideas. In each of your sentences use a different reporting verb or expression. (Some common verbs and expressions are listed in this unit.)

(b) After writing your three sentences, rewrite each one using a different reporting verb or expression.

Example, reporting the same information in different ways:

Vespa asserts that the number twelve is a better basis for   mathematics than ten.

The number twelve, in the opinion of Vespa, is a better basis for mathematics than ten.

According to Vespa, the number twelve is a better basis for mathematics than ten.

Exercise 3

Introductions and Conclusions

Read the following introduction and conclusion of a research paper by Kanyanit Luengransun on the subject of the relationship between music and mathematics. (The body of the paper is not included here.) Answer the questions.

Kanyanit's introduction

Many people think that music, the queen of the arts, and mathematics, the queen of the sciences, are not similar. Some people learn trigonometric functions in school and know what the graph of $y =$

sin x is. Moreover, they know about ratios and mathematical progressions. They think that these are part of physics, astronomy, chemistry, and other sciences. However, Lawlis asserts (1967, p. 593) that intuitive awareness of a relation between music and mathematics existed as early as Pythagoras, a Greek mathematician and philosopher who lived about 500 years B.C. Lawlis investigated the acoustical basis of music through mathematical ratios. Many mathematicians are now interested in the subtle relations and analogies that exist between music and mathematics. Even though most people believe mathematics is only related to sciences, some aspects of mathematical forms are akin to musical forms. This paper will show that music can be expressed as a sine curve, ratios, and mathematical progressions. Furthermore, the harmonic series of both can be shown to be the same.

Kanyanit's conclusion

In summary, music and mathematics have a kinship based on at least four aspects. Both follow the basic idea of mathematical closure of properties, which can be expressed in ratio form; a musical tone is similar to a sine curve; arithmetic progressions in music correspond to geometric progressions in mathematics; and the musical harmonic series is the same as the mathematical harmonic series. The opinion of most people that music and mathematics are not related must, therefore, be changed by the evidence presented here. They do have similarities. However, we also have to remember that, no matter how much mathematicians can connect them, music as art and mathematics as science are different in their purposes.

Introduction

(a) Which sentences give the general context for the paper?

(b) What is the thesis statement of this paper?

(c) Which sentences indicate the main issues to be covered in the body of the paper? What are these issues?

Conclusion

(d) Which sentence restates the key idea expressed in the paper's thesis statement?

(e) Which sentence summarizes the main points that are covered in the body of the paper? What are the points?

(f) There is a reference in the conclusion to the general context provided in the introduction. What is that reference?

Unit 15
Final Draft

The final draft of a research paper for an academic course is the end result of a long process. It is always possible to make the process continue indefinitely, because no piece of writing is ever really complete; it could always be improved in some way. Yet the practical limitations of having to write a paper in only one term make it necessary for the writer to compromise. There is no time to continue rewriting. So at this stage try to be satisfied with what you have.

After writing out the final draft, with major and minor revisions of content and organization, edit your paper for mechanical errors—spelling, grammar, paragraphing, punctuation, and word choice.

THE FINAL EDITING PROCESS

Your goal now is not to make any major revisions but only to edit for formal correctness and best word choice. The kind of reading you do for this purpose is very different from the normal reading that you do for comprehension of books and articles. Reading for editing can be quite unnatural as a reading process.

There are several techniques that writers use for this final editing (also called proofreading) of their paper. Try each one with short sections of your paper to see which you prefer. Choose the one that helps you to locate errors most efficiently.

If you have time before the due date for your final draft, wait two or three days before your final check of the paper because it is easy to miss errors when the writing is still fresh in your mind; waiting for a while will make it seem a little less familiar when you edit, and you will be more likely to catch any errors.

Editing Techniques

1. The most usual technique is to read very slowly through your paper, paying little attention to overall meaning and concentrating instead on separate sentences and individual words. The more slowly you read, the better.

2. Read one line at a time while covering all other lines with a sheet of paper, so that you see only the line being read.

3. Read the paper aloud to yourself because reading aloud forces you to slow down and give more attention to each word.

4. Read the paper sentence by sentence starting from the last sentence (strange as it seems!) and working backward through the whole paper; this reverse reading forces you to focus on the grammar of each sentence separately.

LOOKING AHEAD

To reach this stage of your paper, editing a final draft, you have had to work through many different assignments in this book, starting with the initial search for an idea. Each step is something you have had to think about carefully and do deliberately, with assistance from your instructor in many phases. As you get more practice in writing such papers, you will not have to take each step so deliberately. The stages of this complex process will become habitual and will flow into each other.

In your academic courses, when you hand in the final draft, your instructor will assume that all the steps have been taken, since without them a good paper cannot be produced. In most academic courses, the final draft is the only thing that the instructor sees. In a few courses, however, there may be some guidance, especially in the selection and limitation of a topic. A preliminary thesis statement and outline may be asked for by the instructor, or this may be requested in the form of a statement of the "problem" (the narrowed topic) and its "rationale" (the reason for investigating this topic). Very rarely is any further help routinely given to all students in a class, but instructors are generally willing to discuss individual research problems as they arise. In many colleges it is also possible to get help with writing problems from departments variously referred to as "Writing Workshop," "Writing Center," "Writing Lab," "Study Skills Center," and so on. Do not hesitate to approach such centers (which normally provide their help at no charge). The experienced tutors there have come across most kinds of research and writing difficulty and will be able to help you.

Your best help, however, will come from going through the research paper composing process several times in the manner suggested by this guidebook: think initially of the aim of the whole paper and then break down the process of completing it into a series of manageable stages, corresponding to the sequence of assignments given here. In this way you are less likely to find the process overwhelming. It may remain difficult, because writing in any language, native or foreign, is usually difficult and demanding, but you will be confident that your difficulties and problems are part of the process for everyone and not yours alone. Overcoming these research and writing difficulties, learning more about your subject, becoming an expert in your topic, and completing the research paper are the personal satisfactions to be gained from seeing the process through from beginning to end.

If you have reached this point in this book, step by step, you have traveled a long way! Congratulations, and polish that final draft carefully before relaxing!

Unit 16
Format of a Research Paper in APA Style

Providing reference citations and a bibliography is often referred to as "documenting sources." The purpose of this is to allow your readers, if they wish, to find the documents you have used. They may want to do so because of interest in the topic or because they want to see how you have made use of the sources. A second reason for documenting is to make full acknowledgment of the sources you have used. This reason is tied to the issue of plagiarism. Any ideas you use that are not your own must be acknowledged, just as you must acknowledge any phrases, sentences, or special uses of words that you get from your sources. Ideas or terms that have become widely current in a field, to the extent that it would be impossible to track down the "owner" or originator of them, do not need to be acknowledged.

There are different ways of citing references according to different style guides and different disciplines. The one used in this book, following the APA style, is author/date documentation. In this system, the citations are given in parentheses immediately following the information to be acknowledged. The reader can then go to the reference list for the publication and title details. (In other systems, citations are given as footnotes at the bottom of each page or as footnotes on a separate page at the end of the paper. When they are on a separate page at the end they may also be referred to as "endnotes" or simply "notes.")

The information given here, adapted from the APA manual, is adequate for most student papers. It is, however, far from complete. For further details, consult the manual itself.

QUOTATIONS

Short quotations (up to four lines) are made part of the text and are enclosed in double quotation marks.

Longer quotations are indented five spaces as a block, with no quotation marks. Continue to double-space lines in a block quotation.

For all quotations, cite author, year, and page number(s). In parentheses include information not mentioned in the text; for instance, if the author's name is in the text, there is no need to repeat it in parentheses.

Three ellipsis points (. . .) indicate words omitted from within a sentence. Four ellipsis points show omission of words between sentences.

Use square brackets to enclose material that is not part of the original quotation.

Within double quotation marks, use single quotation marks for quoted material or words that would otherwise be in double quotation marks. Within a block quotation use double quotation marks.

Here are three examples:

Quotation 1.

She comments, "The test results are 'contaminated' . . . because of influence from the way it was administered" (Lee, 1984, p. 63).

Quotation 2.

According to Lee (1984), "the test results are 'contaminated'" (p. 63) due to faulty administrative procedures.

Quotation 3.

Lee (1984) makes the following comments about the tests:
> The experimenters allowed them [the candidates] to work with all the questions before the day of the experiment. They should have allowed half of the candidates to work with the first set of questions, and the other half to work with the second set. The test results are "contaminated" . . . because of influence from the way it was administered (p. 63).

REFERENCE CITATIONS

Cite the author's last name, the year of publication, and, whenever possible, the page numbers. Place in parentheses only what is not mentioned in the text, as in these examples:

Lee (1981) states that there are . . .

It has recently been claimed (Lee, 1979) that there are . . .

Sometimes both year and date are in the text, and so nothing is added in parentheses:

In 1968, Lee denied that there are . . .

With page numbers, the above three examples would appear like this:

Lee (1981, p. 76) states that there are . . .

It has recently been claimed (Lee, 1979, pp. 22–24) that there are . . .

In 1968, Lee (pp. 201–202) denied that there are . . .

When there are two authors, give both names every time they are cited. Where there are more than two authors, give all the authors' names when they are first cited; thereafter, give only the first author's name and add "et al." For example, a first citation might be:

As Gonzalez, al-Ali, Chang, and Jones (1966) noted, it is true that . . .

and a later citation of the same work would be:

Gonzalez et al. further explained how subjects would . . .

When one author has published more than one work in the same year, add the letters a, b, c, and so on, to the year in the reference citation and to the year in the listing of these items in the reference list:

According to Waleski (1997b, p. 602), children try to . . .

When citing someone indirectly (mentioned in another source), use one of these formats:

Jones (1997, p. 26) quotes Smith as stating . . .

Smith (quoted by Jones, 1997, p. 26) states . . .

Smith is cited by Jones (1997, p. 26) as stating . . .

When citing more than one author for the same publication, do the following (adapted from the APA's more detailed guidelines): for a work with two authors, always cite both names; for a work with more than two authors, cite only the name of the first author followed by "et al.", as in these examples:

> In the view of some researchers (Mead and Jones, 1997, pp. 213–217) the best solution is to . . .

> The results are ambiguous, as some have noted (Franco, et al.).

Even though the "et al." abbreviation is used in in-text citations, the bibliography must list all the authors of each publication.

BIBLIOGRAPHY OR REFERENCES?

The APA manual recommends that the word *references* be used for works that directly support a paper and that the word *bibliography* be used for a list including background or further reading. So, if you use the heading "References," everything in the list must be mentioned somewhere in the text, and everything mentioned in the text must appear in the list. If you use the heading "Bibliography," you may add to the list some items that are not directly referred to in the text.

For the format of entries in a bibliography, refer to the earlier section on preparing a preliminary bibliography. In addition, do the following:

> Alphabetize the entries, but do not number them.

> Double-space between lines, starting the first line of each entry at the margin and indenting additional lines of each entry.

FOOTNOTES

Footnotes may explain or amplify material in the text, but they are distracting to a reader. Whenever possible this information should be made part of the text. When used, footnotes appear after the reference list. Such footnotes are numbered and are referred to in the text by a raised (superscript) number, for example:

Three experts were consulted for their opinions.[14] Then we . . .

TABLES

Use tables if they help to make the written information clearer without just repeating that information. The table number and heading are placed at the top left of the table. Here is an example:

Table 12
Number of Correct Selections Made by Each Color Group

	Color Group			
Experiment	Red	Green	Blue	Yellow
1	26	22	31	19
2	25	42	30	28
3	13	16	33	12

Tables should be included in the text of the paper. For student papers, it is more convenient to place the table on a separate page in the text, which should be included in the page numbering of the paper.

FIGURES

In APA style, the term *figure* is used for any illustration other than a table. (Figures cannot be typed; tables can be typed.) Use figures only if they help to support the text. As with tables, include them in the text, but, for convenience in a student paper, place them on a separate, numbered page. The figure number and caption are placed at the bottom of the graph or illustration, as in this example:

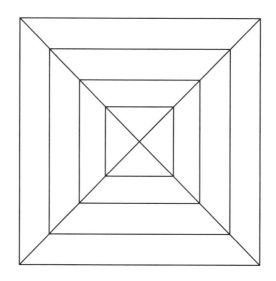

Figure 3. Perceptual variation: Does this represent a view looking down onto a solid object with steps on the outside, or a view into a hollow object with steps on the inside?

PAGE NUMBERING

Use arabic numerals in the top right-hand corner for page numbering. Start counting with the cover page, but do not write the page number on it. The numbers are written on all other pages, including the first page of the text.

HEADINGS AND SUBHEADINGS IN THE TEXT

In a student paper, it is usually not necessary to use headings and sub-headings in the text although in some technical and scientific papers they are frequently used. Such headings must not be a substitute for transitional sentences and paragraphs. Use them only if they are usual in papers in your subject area. In a short paper, headings such as "Intro-duction" and "Conclusion" are of no real use because it is assumed that the first few paragraphs are introductory and the last few are conclud-ing. If you do use headings in the text, center and underline them, like this:

<u>A centered heading</u>

Unit 17
Example:
A Student's
Research Paper

The extracts in this unit are from a student's research paper. Her paper follows the style of the *Publication Manual of the American Psychological Association,* 4th ed. (1994). Comments have been placed in the margin to draw attention to various aspects of format and style.

Only the beginning and ending pages of the paper are presented here to provide examples of format; the middle pages are omitted.

When writing your paper:

Use 8½ by 11-inch sheets of paper.

Leave a margin of 1–1½ inches at the left, right, top, and bottom of each page.

Write only on one side of each sheet.

Double-space (leave a blank line) between all lines of the text.

The Shadow Side of Plastic Packaging

in the United States

Dagmar Kamecke

Course: _____

Instructor: _____

Date: _____

The cover page includes title, author, course number, instructor's name, date.

Center the title on the page.

Capitalize the initial letters of important words (not articles and prepositions) in the title.

If the title is more than one line, double-space between lines.

Place the author's name, centered, a few lines below the title.

Place the remaining information, also centered, lower on the page.

The cover page is counted in page numbering, but the number is not written on the page.

Start writing page numbers on the second page, in the top right hand corner.

The Shadow Side of Plastic Packaging

in the United States

Repeat the title at the beginning of the thesis statement and outline page(s).

Thesis Statement

Although the recycling of plastic packaging in the United States can diminish the plastic waste stream, the excessive use of plastic packaging is difficult to justify from an environmental as well as from an economic point of view.

Write the thesis statement at the top of the page, after the subheading Thesis Statement.

Outline:

I.   The use of plastic packaging in the United States

    A.   Extent and trends

    B.   Explanations

        i.   Characteristics of plastic

        ii.   Social changes

        iii. High marketability

II. Environmental consequences of the disposal of plastic packaging

    A.   Impact on landfills

    B.   Effects of incineration

III. Recycling of plastic packaging for environmental relief

    A.   Kinds of recyclability

        i.   Bringing back to original use

        ii.   Producing other goods

Write the outline below the thesis statement, after the subheading Outline.

In the outline, indicate the comparative importance of different parts by using indentation, roman numerals, capital letters, and arabic numerals.

           iii.   Creating fuel or chemicals

           iv.   Recovering energy by incineration

     B.   Legal aspects

     C.   Extent of recycling and current trends

IV.   Economic evaluation of the use of plastic packaging

     A.   Most efficient distribution of the
           real costs and incentives

     B.   Actual distribution of the real costs
           and incentives

The Shadow Side of Plastic Packaging
in the United States

The United States is confronted with a tremendous postconsumer waste stream, the disposal of which is increasingly difficult to handle. "The solid waste crisis is real" (Brewer, 1988, p. 109). The growing amount of plastic, especially of waste from plastic packaging, contributes to a large extent to this problem. Although the recycling of plastic packaging in the United States can diminish the plastic waste stream, the excessive use of plastic packaging is difficult to justify from an environmental as well as from an economic point of view. To understand this issue, we first need to analyze the increasing extent of the use of plastic packaging and the environmental effects of its disposal. Then, an analysis of the recycling of plastic packaging will show the potential of recycling for environmental relief. The economic analysis that follows is based on the consideration of the real costs of plastic packaging because the actual distribution of these costs must be contrasted with the economically efficient distribution of the costs. Also, the impact of incentives affects the costs.

It should be understood first that the increasing use of plastic in many kinds of applications is a national trend in the United States. The highest growth rate, however, is the use of plastic packaging. Between 1977 and 1987 it almost tripled

Write the title at the beginning of the first page of text.

Leave a space of a few lines between the title and the first paragraph.

Quotation, with citation

Indent paragraphs, including the first one. Do not leave a blank line between paragraphs.

The thesis statement appears in the introduction. This tells the reader, at the beginning, the main point of the paper.

The last part of the introduction mentions, in order, the main parts of the discussion that follows in the whole paper. This helps the reader to know how the paper is organized.

(Stephens, 1987, p. 111) and created about 45 to 50 percent of the postconsumer plastic waste. The development of new plastic packaging materials has been very intensive (Wolf, 1991, p. 16) because plastic has been increasingly replacing traditional packaging materials like glass, metals and paper (Wolf, 1991, p. 5). One survey showed that 50 percent of all product packaging of a supermarket and 40 percent of that of a drugstore were entirely made of plastic, whereas only 1.3 percent, 3.9 percent and 12.1 percent of the drugstore products were entirely packaged in paper, glass and cardboard (Wolf, 1991, p. 6). Because of the rapid progress in the development of plastic packaging, it is possible to use plastic in a growing number of applications, especially in the area of food packaging. Examples are the switch from glass milk bottles to high density polyethylene (HDPE) bottles, and from glass containers for beverages, peanut butter and mustard to polyethylene teraphthalate (PET) containers (Wolf, 1991, pp. 29-30). Furthermore, a considerable amount of excess packaging contributes to the proliferation of plastic packaging. These trends towards an excessive use of plastic packaging are predicted to keep on growing fast in the future (Selke, 1988, p. 59).

What has caused this trend in packaging? The answer is in three very different things coming together: the qualities of plastic, certain social changes, and the easy marketing of plastic.

The superior characteristics of plastic compared with other packaging materials are less weight, unbreakability, durability and

Citation

Citation

Citation

Citation

Citation

Transition word between sentences

Citation

Transition paragraph

microwaveability. How could these features cause a shift in packaging towards plastic? On the consumer side these features have been very welcomed, because of a combination of social changes and technological developments. Families have become smaller and typically both partners are working. Furthermore, the number of elderly people has increased, and a different lifestyle is developing, which is also caused to a certain extent by these changes. Consequently, a new kind of demand was born: the demand for quick, convenient, and clean consumption, which in addition must be secure against tampering and easy to dispose of. Combined with the technology of the microwave, which can be found in most American homes, the desired packaging features were quite obvious.

Transition word between sentences

People prefer to buy the products with lighter packages, especially in the case of beverage containers, and they choose food packages which they can put immediately into the microwave. Also, single packages are very important because of a rather individualistic lifestyle and the elderly people's needs. These containers may also function as dishes, so one has to put them into the garbage after consumption. Compared to the traditional cooking, this saves a lot of time and effort, but it has also led to a further proliferation of plastic packaging. Because of the high marketability of this type of packaging, the packaging designers concentrated on the search for further applications for plastics whereby they could increase their opportunities with new

Transition word between sentences

types of plastics. For the manufacturers of consumer products, plastic packaging was a cheap alternative. They saved transportation costs because of the lesser weight of plastic and they have less loss by breakage in the production process (Wolf, 1991, p. 5; pp. 31-32). Plastic packaging has a lot of advantages, but when it enters the waste stream, its advantages turn into an environmental threat.

Citation

This threat is a result of difficulty in disposal of the waste. Today the main means of disposal are landfill and incineration. Each has several impacts on the environment. One of the main problems of landfills is that plastic does not degrade. Because of its large volume, plastic packaging takes a large amount of space in the landfill. It is not biodegradable, so it hinders efficient decomposition which would enable a longer lifespan for the landfill. Thus plastic contributes to the landfill capacity problems by requiring a lot of space and by shortening the lifespan of the landfills. An estimate by the Environmental

Transition sentence

Transition word between sentences.

!!!
THE MIDDLE PAGES OF THIS PAPER HAVE BEEN OMITTED
!!!

Since 1986, the developments in the recycling technology have been concentrated on improvements of existing technologies instead of developing new recycling technologies. Furthermore, according to Curlee (1989, p. 196) the developments were focused rather on plastic waste, which is based on only one type of plastic, and clean commingled plastic waste. One notable exception is the recent development reported in *Business Week* of a process to break the plastic down into the original molecular blocks (April 14, 1991, p. 72). The potential of this technology and its separation requirements are difficult to evaluate. Beyond all the problems of plastic packaging recycling, the euphoria about the alternative of the development of degradable plastic has slowed down the recycling efforts to a certain extent (Curlee, 1989, p. 210). However, "the vast majority of plastic continues to enter the municipal waste stream ..." (Curlee, 1989, p. 20). The environmental relief by recycling seems in general to be overestimated so that plastic packaging should be used with care.

A proper consideration, however, should take an economic viewpoint into account. Aside from the fact that it is economically questionable to use non-renewable resources for throwaway products, the following economic evaluation of the use of plastic packaging is based on the consideration of the real costs of recycling. Beyond the production costs of plastic packaging, the real cost also includes the cost of disposal. The costs are distributed among the manufacturers, the consumers, and the

Citation

Citation

Citation

Quotation, with citation

communities. An economically efficient distribution requires that the ones who cause the costs have to bear them. Whenever this condition is not satisfied, the economic incentives will be weakened and lead to an inefficient outcome.

Actually, the production costs are a part of the price which the consumers have to pay, but the disposal costs are borne by the communities. The costs of landfill and incineration were considerable. While incineration in 1984 cost between $8.66 and $ 22.77 per ton, the landfill costs ranged between $6.98 and $15.33 per ton. However, especially the costs for landfill disposal grew drastically and account for up to $150 per ton in certain communities in 1987. Shrinking landfill capacity accompanied by exploding disposal costs created a strong incentive for the communities to support recycling and the avoidance of plastic waste. Because neither the manufacturers nor the consumers have to bear the real costs of the use of plastic as packaging material, both have no economic incentive to reduce the use of plastic. Although the consumers bear indirectly a certain amount of the costs through the general tax, this is not connected with their consumption, so it does not affect the buying decision.

As soon as the price of plastic packaging would reflect the real costs, the use of plastic packaging would be drastically reduced. When the manufacturers have to pay the real costs, they would shift them to the consumer, so that it would be equal to the situation in which the consumer has to pay the cost. The

Transition word between paragraphs

Transition word between sentences.

110

consumer would then switch to cheaper alternatives or reduce his consumption until his willingness to pay, which reflects his appreciation of the advantages of plastic packaging, will equal the price. The resulting decrease of the demand would change the packaging strategies on the supply side. The use of plastic packaging will be smaller than in the actual distribution of the real costs.

The difference between the actual plastic packaging use and the possible use in the most efficient way can be considered as the excessive part of the use of plastic packaging. One step towards an efficient allocation of the costs can be seen in the packaging taxes in certain states. These taxes were differentiated according to the recyclability of the packaging. However, this kind of tax is not yet enough.

To conclude, the greatly increasing use of plastic, especially in packaging, has been met with attempts to diminish the plastic waste stream by recycling. This has had some effect, but it remains difficult to dispose of plastic completely. There are still bad effects on the environment. In addition, from the viewpoint of economics, the cost of plastic packaging is not only in the packaging. It is also costly to dispose of. Therefore, neither the environmental nor the economic analyses give any justification for the excessive use of plastic packaging. In the end, all the consequences of the current use are shifted to the future generations.

The last few paragraphs form the conclusion.

The concluding paragraph briefly mentions the main points of the paper.

The conclusion restates, in different words, the claim expressed in the thesis statement that is in the introduction.

Bibliography

Albertsson, A., & Huang, S. J. (Eds.) (1995). *Degradable polymers, recycling, and plastics waste management.* New York: Dekker.

Brewer, G. (1988, June). *Plastic recycling initiatives in New England.* Paper presented at the Recyclingplas III - Conference of the Plastics Institute of America, Washington, DC.

Brewer, G. (1989). Plastic recycling action plan for Massachusetts, Part 1. *Journal of Environmental Systems, 18,* pp. 213-264.

Curlee, T. R. (1987, June). *The economic feasibility of plastic recycling.* Paper presented at the Recyclingplas II - Conference of the Plastics Institute of America, Washington, DC.

Curlee, T. R. (1988-89). The feasibility of recycling plastic wastes: An update. *Journal of Environmental Systems, 18,* pp. 193-212.

Kibbel, H. (No date). Project-216: The current status of plastics recycling. Available: http://alpha.vyne.com/bcc/plasticspolym/P216.html

Marbach, W. D. (1991, April 14). Plastic can be just as strong the second time around. *Business Week,* p. 72.

Selke, S. E. (1988, June). *Recycling of plastic packaging.* Paper presented at the Recyclingplas III - Conference of the Plastics Institute of America, Washington, DC.

Wolf, N. A., & Feldman, E. (1991). *Plastics: America's packaging dilemma.* Washington, DC: Island Press.

Start the Bibliography or References list on a new page.

Center the heading.

"Bibliography" (not "References") is used as the heading for this paper because some items listed are not directly mentioned in the paper.

The first line of each entry is not indented. After the first line, indent each line five spaces (or the same amount as a paragraph indent).

For on-line electronic references, do not add a period at the end of the entry.

Double space between all lines of the Bibliography.

Unit 18

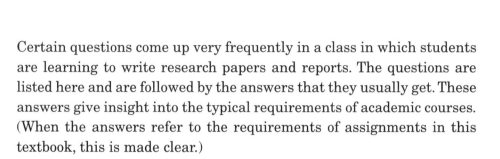

Frequent Student Questions

Certain questions come up very frequently in a class in which students are learning to write research papers and reports. The questions are listed here and are followed by the answers that they usually get. These answers give insight into the typical requirements of academic courses. (When the answers refer to the requirements of assignments in this textbook, this is made clear.)

1. How long should my paper be?

To this question, many instructors give the vague answer: "As long as it needs to be in order to say what you have to say." This leaves inexperienced student writers puzzled because they usually think that a paper is not a research paper if it is very short. In fact, academic research papers and reports vary greatly in length, from "short" (1–6 pages of double-spaced typescript) to "medium" (7–15 pages) to "long" (15–40 pages). If your instructor does not give you upper and lower page limits, then you should think in terms of a medium length paper. A very short student paper is unlikely to be thorough and complete, and a very long one will not be impressive just because it is long. The most effective paper is both complete and concise.

2. How much note-taking must I do?

There is no specific quantity that is best. In academic courses, the instructor never sees your notes, so you can write them as you wish, and you can write as much or as little as you wish. As a rough guideline, it may help you to think that a typical medium-length paper (7–15 pages) will be based on 30 to 50 pages of notes, but this varies a lot according to the subject, the writer, and the books and articles the writer has immediately at hand when actually writing.

You should always think of note-taking as having three equally im-portant purposes: the obvious one of recording information and the two that are sometimes forgotten—writing notes helps you understand and organize information in your mind, and it also stimulates your own ideas.

3. Must my paper be typed?

You should type your paper unless the instructor gives special permis-sion not to do so. If you handwrite a paper, be sure it is easy to read. Do not put the reader in the position of having to struggle to read your handwriting. The easier it is to read, the happier your instructor will be! Instructors are influenced, even if only subconsciously, by untidy or illegible presentation and layout—including handwriting. Graduate stu-dents are expected to type all their papers. Always find out exactly what each instructor wants.

4. I've seen some students hand in their papers in plastic covers with bindings. Is this necessary?

No. The fancy cover makes no difference to the quality of the writing and research. A simple cover sheet is enough. However, you may believe that there could be a subconscious influence on the reader if your paper has a special, fancy cover. Think about it and decide for yourself!

5. How many books and articles must I use for my paper?

There is no "must" on this issue. Some research papers use many, others very few. Some papers refer only to articles. Others refer only to books, but, if the papers are up to date, they usually include references to some recent articles as well as to books. For some papers that report experi-mental results in scientific fields, there may be no references at all, but this is rare because such results are usually presented in the context of previously published research. For the type of student paper discussed in this textbook, there should probably be a minimum of about four or five references to books or articles.

6. Does this textbook contain all I need in order to write pa-pers for my academic courses in the correct format?

No, it does not. There is probably enough here for most undergraduate papers, but graduate students should obtain a copy of the style guide required for their specialized areas, especially when they are getting close to writing their theses or dissertations. Find out from your professors what the preferred style guides are.

7. How do I know which editorial style to use—APA or MLA or scientific or some other?

Ask your academic advisor or course professors or advanced graduate students in your subject area what the standard requirements are.

8. How many spaces should I leave between lines?

When typing it is customary to double-space, and when handwriting you should leave one line blank after each line of writing. This makes it easier for the instructor to read and also leaves space for the instructor to write comments.

9. Should I write on both sides of each sheet of paper?

Use one side only. Even if you are allowed to handwrite your paper, writing on one side is usually easier for the reader, and it also has an advantage for you. As you write, you are sure to make mistakes or change your mind about some things as you go along—a normal part of writing; if you write on one side only, you will not have to rewrite as much as you would if you were using both sides.

10. Should the thesis statement be part of the paper or just written separately on a separate page at the beginning?

It must be part of the text of the paper. It is a sentence that appears in one of the introductory paragraphs. When you write the thesis statement on a separate page (as in the sequence of assignments in this textbook), that is only a convenience for the instructor. In your academic courses there is no need to write it on a separate page unless your instructor specifically asks for it. When the instructor requires an abstract (or summary, or outline) at the beginning of the paper, the thesis statement is normally included in it.

11. Must every paper have an outline at the beginning on a separate sheet, like the "contents" page of a book, to help the reader?

An outline with numbering and indentation is not normally part of a research paper that you hand in to an instructor in an academic course.

In this textbook it was required so that your writing instructor could see how you had organized your paper. In your academic courses, present a separate outline or abstract only if it is requested. The way you have organized the parts and arguments of your paper should always be stated in the introductory paragraphs, where you should write several sentences to explain this. So, in a way, your outline is in the introduction, but it appears as consecutive sentences in a paragraph and not as the indented and numbered outline that you can use to help organize your thoughts during the writing process. Letting your reader know the structure of your paper in this way is an essential aid to him or her in setting up a mental framework within which to understand what you have written. In short, you write separate outlines for yourself to structure and develop your own thoughts, and you place an "outline" in the mind of your reader as part of the introduction.

12. I don't like to write detailed outlines with indentation and numbering, so why should I do so?

You do not have to write formal outlines when producing a paper for your academic courses. In that situation, no one except you would see such an outline.

The outline is intended only as a guide to you in your own thinking and writing. A few, very rare writers are able to keep a clear organization in their minds and not write outlines as they go along, but most of us are not like that. Also, writing down your ideas has a different effect from just thinking about how to organize them. Writing them down triggers other ideas; rereading what you have written also sets new possibilities going in the mind; and a simple renumbering is a quick way to try out new arrangements of ideas. Instead of thinking of outlining as a burden, think of it as the beginning of drafting your paper.

Sometimes, an instructor will want to see a formal outline, but in such a case it will be requested. If the formal outline is to be handed in with the final draft, then you can leave its final version till last: write it only after you have completed the final draft. All other outlines are really just temporary things that assist you in the process of writing. They are not ends in themselves.

In the sequence of assignments in this book, your preliminary outline and a revised version of it are asked for only so that your instructor can see how you are proceeding with your ongoing ideas about the paper. Also it gets you going with thinking and writing, instead of allow-ing too much time to pass (as it so easily can) in note-taking alone and in vague and unfocused thinking.

13. When should I use quotations? Must I always use some or can I write a research paper without using any at all?

You should only quote something directly when the way it is expressed is especially effective or unusual. Quotations are not some kind of decoration or a required part of a student paper. Indeed you may have *no* need for *any* quotations. Many research papers that report experimental results do not have quotations, but papers in the humanities and social sciences usually do because they deal very often with the ideas of other writers. To decide whether to paraphrase or quote directly just ask yourself if you are more interested in *what* is said than *how* it is said. If it is the content (what is said) that you are interested in, then paraphrase. If it is the manner of expression (how it is said) that is striking, then quote directly. Never quote too much (not more than about ten percent of a paper), or your instructor might begin to think that you are using quotations just to fill pages!

14. Must every paper prove something?

No. Only an argumentative paper tries to prove a point. Other papers — reports — do not try to gather evidence and use logical argument to support a claim that some people might disagree with. When you begin a research paper project, you should have an absolutely clear idea of which type is required of you. Often, undergraduates must write reports, but it is rare for graduate students to do so. The normal requirement for graduates is to write argumentative papers. If you are in doubt about what you have to do, discuss it with your instructor early in the term.

15. What is the difference between the "thesis" of an argument and the use of the word *thesis* in "thesis statement" and in "graduate thesis"?

You have to be careful in using the term *thesis*. It has two basic meanings: one is "a proposition presented for discussion or proof"; the second meaning (derived from the first) is "a written dissertation required by a college as part of the work toward a higher degree."

The thesis of an argument is the proposition that the argument is trying to prove; it is the claim that is being supported through evidence and logical statements. This is the meaning in the phrase *thesis state-*

ment in this textbook, referring to the one sentence that expresses the main idea of a research paper.

It is also possible to use the phrase *thesis statement* more loosely to mean several sentences that express both a summarized argument and the point that the argument is trying to make. This looser usage sometimes appears in dissertations in a section headed "Statement of the Thesis," but, strictly defined, the "thesis statement" is only the assertion that is to be proved and not the argumentation that leads to proof.

In the context of a single research paper, the "thesis statement" is synonymous with "thesis sentence," a single, grammatically complete sentence, the main clause of which expresses the idea to be proved or expanded upon.

When talking of a "graduate thesis," reference is being made to the written dissertation previously defined.

16. What can I do if I find it impossible to remember all the rules for citation formats?

Do not even try to remember them. All writers of such papers keep style guides for reference, and these are normally used at the end of the whole writing process. That is, you can put your citations in the correct format after you have written the text of the paper. The format and the "look" of the paper should not be in your mind when you are busy developing ideas, drafting and redrafting. Thinking about the mechanical conventions at this point would only interfere with the flow of activity. However, when you are developing a preliminary bibliography, be sure to note all the information that you will need for a complete citation, so that you will not waste time later, when you can least afford the time, in going back to the library just to get such simple information.

17. Should I leave out information that I think the instructor knows?

Even though the actual writing situation is that of student and instructor, you should not try to guess what an individual instructor may or may not know. Rather, imagine that you are writing for readers who are knowledgeable about your general subject but not about the details of your narrowed topic. With this guideline in mind, you will avoid writing too much that is obvious or leaving out some information that is needed.

Your reading about the general subject area will tell you what is widely known, and your reading within the narrowed topic area will tell you what very few people are thinking about and writing about. However, when you become familiar with a very limited topic, you can easily take for granted some things that people need to know, so you should give too much rather than too little background information if you are finding it hard to establish the right balance. Think of the instructor as representing a group of readers, a fairly small community of specialists.

Even in your English language class, in which the instructor obviously cannot be a specialist in all the disciplines of the various students, you should still write your paper as if for a community of experts in your field. Your English instructor will read your paper for how you write it rather than for what you write; the latter is for an academic subject specialist to judge.

18. Am I expected to write papers like those in academic journals while I am still a student?

Your instructors do not expect you to do that, but they do hope that your approach to the whole process of research, thinking, and expressing your ideas will be the same as that of the professional, academic writers. Also, more is naturally expected of graduates than undergraduates. A research paper written for a graduate academic course should really be fairly close to the type and quality of short, published articles.

19. If I know a lot about a subject from my own experience, can I write the research paper from this knowledge, without using books and articles?

No. If you did that, it would not be a research paper in the usual scholarly sense. Certainly you could use your experience of a special field as a source of ideas for a research paper, for instance, for an idea that you want to prove is true or useful or original. That idea would be expressed in your thesis statement. Or you might use personal experience as part of the evidence in an argument but only as a small part because it would be very subjective and, probably, impossible to test scientifically or argue about in a strictly logical way.

If you write from personal experience, you would be writing a personal essay, a composition that would be quite acceptable in another situation (such as a weekly composition for a writing teacher) but not as a research paper.

Using books and articles is an integral part of writing a research paper, especially in the humanities and social sciences. In some scientific fields, papers that report the results of experimental research may make no reference to other works, but even in the scientific papers there is often some attempt to put the information in the context of the work of others.

20. Can I use subheadings in a research paper and, if so, how many?

In a short paper, it is best to avoid all subheadings, unless you are certain that they would help your reader. Using too many can make the paper seem to lack cohesion because they are not a good substitute for effective transitional sentences or paragraphs. The headings "Introduction" and "Conclusion" are often used when they are not really necessary. In a short paper, it does not need to be stated that the first few paragraphs are introductory and the last few concluding because this is assumed. In long papers subheadings are more useful, but there is no way to calculate a number that is appropriate; each must be judged separately. In some technical and scientific fields, it is normal to use specific subheadings for every paper. As you read articles in your field, you will soon notice what is typical, and you can also find out what is suitable from the style guide used in that field.

21. Why are research papers assigned in so many different academic courses?

Research papers are the basis of communication between scholars. You might even think of many academic books as consisting of sets of research papers (or articles or chapters) that develop a subject in depth. The process of writing a research paper—investigation, analysis, developing and changing ideas, clear self-expression in writing, and learning through writing—is a vital part of what colleges and universities are trying to teach you because this process is fundamental to scholarly communication.

Glossary

The terms in this glossary have been selected to assist with terminology commonly met with in research paper writing and library use. Some of the definitions are based on those in the *American Heritage Dictionary of the English Language*.

Words in CAPITAL LETTERS are themselves defined elsewhere in the Glossary.

A

abbreviation　a shortened form of a word or phrase

abstract　a summary of the content of an ARTICLE, sometimes appearing at the beginning of the article and sometimes printed in an INDEX or DATABASE

academic　related to school and schoolwork

acknowledgment　a statement of the SOURCE of an idea; in a RESEARCH PAPER, full acknowledgment is made of the sources of ideas, information, and quotations; without this, one could be accused of PLAGIARISM

afterword　a statement at the end of a composition or text but not part of the main text; similar to ENDNOTE

alphabetical order　sequencing of names or words according to the letters of the alphabet and based on the series of letters in the spelling of the word or name

alphabetize　to arrange in order of the letters of a language; with words or names, the first letter takes priority, followed by the second letter of each, and so on

analysis　in writing, a way of organizing information by separating a whole into its parts; also called DIVISION

annual   a PERIODICAL published each year

anonymous   without a known author

APA   abbreviation of American Psychological Association, which publishes a widely used STYLE GUIDE

appendix   a separate section of supplementary material at the end of a book (plural: *appendixes* or *appendices*)

Arabic numerals   the numerals 1, 2, 3, 4, 5, 6, 7, 8, 9, 0; compare ROMAN NUMERALS

argument   a discussion of opposing points; a process of reasoning; a series of reasons

argumentative research paper   a RESEARCH PAPER that uses EVIDENCE and argumentation to support an assertion made by the author; may be contrasted with a REPORT; see also CRITIQUE

argumentative thesis statement   a THESIS STATEMENT expressing a point of view that opposes other points of view, making a CLAIM or assertion that needs to be supported with EVIDENCE

article   a short, written composition explaining or arguing something; typically published in scholarly PERIODICALS or newspapers; several articles together may be published as a book

assert   to state something as if it is true

assignment   something given as a task

audience   a group of readers, listeners, or spectators; the assumed audience of a RESEARCH PAPER is readers who have a similar background to the writer; the actual audience of a student research paper is the instructor, but the paper is written as if by one authority for other authorities

author   the writer of a paper, composition, essay, book, or other text

author card   in a library, a CATALOG card alphabetized according to the author's last name

author/date documentation   the style of SOURCE DOCUMENTATION that includes author, date, and page references in the body of the text; placed in parentheses, with no separate footnotes; sometimes called IN-TEXT DOCUMENTATION

author number   part of a library book's CALL NUMBER

authority   an expert in a particular field; authorities are often cited in research papers

B

biannual a publication that appears twice in each year; compare BIENNIAL

bibliography a list of works consulted for a book or article, usually placed at the end of it; a list of works on a specific subject; a list of works by one author; for a RESEARCH PAPER, includes works not mentioned specifically in the paper but consulted for background

biennial a publication that appears every two years; compare BIANNUAL

biography a history of someone's life

block INDENTATION of a series of lines in a text; a long QUOTATION is usually blocked, with no quotation marks, to set it off from the rest of the text

block letter same as CAPITAL LETTER

body in a paper, all the text except for the introduction and conclusion

book a written volume by one or many authors; does not refer to a periodical containing short articles by different authors but can refer to a collection of such articles produced as a one-time publication

book number part of a library book's CALL NUMBER; also called the AUTHOR NUMBER

browse to inspect in a leisurely or casual way; often refers to looking at books in a library or bookstore or looking at documents on the INTERNET or WORLD WIDE WEB

C

call number number used to locate a book in a library, normally written on the spine of the book; for academic libraries, usually the LIBRARY OF CONGRESS CLASSIFICATION SYSTEM of numbers is used for assigning numbers

capital letter a letter of the alphabet written in a larger (and sometimes different) form, as compared to its SMALL LETTER; also called an UPPER CASE letter

card catalog a series of files with cards listing information about publications (author, title, subject) and their location in the library; in some libraries, the catalog is in a computer DATABASE, not on cards; see CATALOG

catalog [also spelled "catalogue"] a list of items, sometimes with a brief description of each item; in a library this refers to a list of publications stored in a computer or card system; see CARD CATALOG

cause and effect in writing, a possible way of organizing information [cause = something responsible for a result; effect = a result produced by something]

CD-ROM abbreviation for compact disk Read-Only Memory; a way of storing information or creating DATABASES on compact disks for use with computers; often used in libraries for INDEXES and CATALOGS

centered heading a heading placed in the center of a line; compare SIDE HEADING and PARAGRAPH HEADING

chart in a book or paper, a page on which information is presented in the form of diagrams, graphs, or tables

cite (v) [citation (n)] to identify as an AUTHORITY or example, usually in order to support an ARGUMENT; in a RESEARCH PAPER, citations are references to authors quoted or mentioned and are part of the DOCUMENTATION

claim a statement or assertion of something as a fact

class number part of a library book's CALL NUMBER, indicating which subject area the book falls into

classification in writing, a way of organizing information according to groups with shared features

clause a group of words (containing a subject and a predicate) that forms part of a compound or complex sentence

closed stacks library shelves that are not open directly to borrowers; a library area from which librarians must retrieve books for borrowers; compare OPEN STACKS

coherence in writing, the quality of parts of text being meaningfully connected with each other, even when COHESIVE DEVICES are not used; compare COHESION

cohesion in writing, the quality of having parts of text (such as sentences or paragraphs or sections) connected with each other by means of COHESIVE DEVICES; compare COHERENCE

cohesive devices in writing, units of language—such as transitional words, phrases, sentences, or paragraphs—used to make explicit connections between parts of text

comparison in writing, a way of arranging information by describing similarities and differences; compare CONTRAST

compile (v) [compilation (n)] to gather into one list or book; to collect items from several sources for a list or for a body of information; for example, a bibliographical list may be compiled

composing process the complex mental and physical activities that take place before and during writing; they include PREWRITING, DRAFTING, REVISING, and EDITING; the activities of composing do not follow each other in a straight line and are cyclic, often merging into each other

composition in reference to writing, a short ESSAY; more generally, something made by putting together parts and elements

computerized database a DATABASE that is stored in computer-readable form; available to users in various ways, usually CD-ROM or REMOTE ACCESS

conclusion in an essay or a paper, the final paragraph(s), usually restating the MAIN IDEA, summarizing the main points, or making a proposal

conference proceedings a publication containing in printed form the papers given orally at a meeting of scholars

connectors same as TRANSITIONS

consult to seek information or advice from someone or something; researchers consult sources for information and ideas

context what comes before or after certain words or passages; the context contributes to how the elements of language are interpreted; the same words may have different meanings in different contexts

contrast in writing, a way of arranging information as a type of COMPARISON that emphasizes differences between two or more things

controlling idea in a RESEARCH PAPER, the main idea expressed in the THESIS STATEMENT; the central notion or concept that indicates the scope of a paper

copyright exclusive legal right to publish, sell, or distribute written or artistic work

copyright date the date when a publication was legally registered in copyright; the date of publication listed in a BIBLIOGRAPHY is normally the most recent copyright date if the book has been published in more than one edition

copyright page the page near the front of a book that gives copyright details such as date, publisher, and publishing history

cover page [also: cover sheet] a page attached to the front of a report or paper on which are written the title, author's name, date, and (if for a school course) the instructor's name and course number

critique a review or commentary that carefully evaluates something; the writer expresses personal judgments about the object of the critique and tries to support those judgments with evidence and logical reasoning; compare ARGUMENTATIVE RESEARCH PAPER and REPORT

cross-reference an indication to a reader about further information elsewhere, often signaled by the phrase *see also;* cross-references to related entries often appear in indexes, bibliographies, and footnotes

D

database a comprehensive collection of related pieces of information ("records") arranged for quick access, usually by computer; see COMPUTERIZED DATABASE

date of publication the year in which a publication first appeared, usually the COPYRIGHT date

definition (n) [define (v)] a statement of the meaning of something; formal definition consists of stating the general class (or species) to which something belongs and then stating how it is different from other things in that class; in writing, extended definition is a way of organizing information

Dewey Decimal classification system a way of arranging publications in a library into ten main areas of knowledge, with further subdivisions; used in many public libraries in the United States; compare LIBRARY OF CONGRESS CLASSIFICATION SYSTEM

dictionary a reference list of words, usually published in book form, giving definitions and other information such as pronunciation; a monolingual dictionary is all in one language; a bilingual dictionary gives translation equivalents

discipline a branch of knowledge or learning

discourse verbal expression in speech or writing; long, formal expression in speech or writing

discovery draft the first DRAFT of a COMPOSITION, written in such a way as to allow thoughts and ideas to flow out freely, without being inhibited by giving attention to the MECHANICS of correct spelling and grammar; the purpose is to find or "discover" ideas; see also FREE WRITING and WRITER'S BLOCK

dissertation a long written work on an academic subject; usually refers to such a work written for a university doctoral degree; compare THESIS

division in writing, a way of organizing information by dividing a whole into its parts; also called ANALYSIS

document (n) sheet(s) of paper with written evidence, proof, or information

document (v) [documentation (n)] to ACKNOWLEDGE all sources in writing a paper, often in FOOTNOTES, BIBLIOGRAPHY, and IN-TEXT DOCUMENTATION

double spacing leaving one line blank after every line of writing

draft (n) [draft (v)] any version of a written document; drafting is part of the COMPOSING PROCESS

E

editing (n) [edit (v)] the stage of the COMPOSING PROCESS in which mechanical errors, such spelling or grammar errors, are checked for and corrected

edition all the copies of a publication printed at one time in one form; later editions contain corrections and revisions of earlier ones

editor someone who prepares a document for publication by selecting, revising, correcting, and so on; someone in charge of the policies of all or part of a publishing company or newspaper

ellipsis the leaving out of part of a sentence, usually marked by ellipsis points (three successive periods [. . .]

encyclopedia a reference work with articles on many subjects; students often start with an encyclopedia when seeking information on a possible RESEARCH PAPER topic

endnote a brief written comment placed at the end of a text, but not forming part of the text itself; similar to AFTERWORD

entry all the information about an item in an INDEX, BIBLIOGRAPHY, DATABASE, or other list

ERIC abbreviation of Educational Resources Information Center; see MICROFORM

essay a short written composition, usually from the author's point of view and usually literary in style

evidence the information on which a proof or judgment is based; an ARGUMENTATIVE RESEARCH PAPER must provide evidence in support of the claim it makes

exposition (n) [expository (adj)] a clear presentation of facts and argument; papers written for academic purposes, such as research papers, are expository in style

extract part of a written composition; something taken out of a larger unit, such as a quotation from a text

F

family name in an English language environment, the LAST NAME or SUR-NAME; alphabetization in a BIBLIOGRAPHY, INDEX, or CATALOG is based on the family name

file card small sheet of stiff paper used to note bibliographic information and keep it systematically; also sometimes used in a system for taking NOTES when writing a RESEARCH PAPER

final draft the version of a written work that is the end product of the COMPOSING PROCESS; the DRAFT that a student hands in to an instructor or that an author sends to a publisher

focus in a paper, the main point of interest expressed in a THESIS STATEMENT; each paragraph and section also has a focus, which may be expressed in a topic sentence

footnote a note placed at the bottom of a page of writing or at the end of a paper, containing a reference or a comment

foreword a statement or introductory note at the beginning of a text but not part of the main text; often gives information about how and why the text was written; a PREFACE

formal language a style of expression that pays careful attention to correct forms and accepted conventions or rules; a RESEARCH PAPER is written in formal language style (in contrast to the informal style of casual conversation)

format the visual layout, size, and shape of a publication; a plan for arranging parts of something in relation to other parts

free writing writing without pause for several minutes, aiming to let ideas flow freely from the mind without being blocked by thinking about mechanics (spelling, grammar, punctuation, format); used as a PREWRITING technique or when the writer has WRITER'S BLOCK; see also DISCOVERY DRAFT

G

gazetteer geographic dictionary or index

given name a person's name other than the FAMILY NAME or SURNAME, usually given to a child by parents at birth; sometimes called the "first name"; the given name is never used to ALPHABETIZE names in a bibliography or index except when there are identical surnames

glossary a collection of specialized terms, with explanation of their meanings in the specialized context

graph a visual display of how two sets of numbers are related to each other, for example, a bar graph or line graph

H

handwriting writing done with the hand; the characteristic writing of a particular person; research papers are usually typed, not handwritten

heading word, phrase, or statement at the beginning of a section of writing, such as a chapter heading; headings are usually marked visually with underlining or a different size or kind of type; see CENTERED HEADING, SIDE HEADING, PARAGRAPH HEADING

humanities philosophy, literature, and fine arts; contrast SOCIAL SCIENCES and SCIENCES

I

illustration clarification by use of example or picture; an explanatory example, picture, photograph, or diagram

indent [indentation (n)] to start a line of writing some way in from the margin; the first line of a PARAGRAPH is usually indented; all the lines of a long quotation are indented, forming a separate BLOCK

index an ALPHABETIZED list of names, places, and subjects, giving information (such as page numbers) to help in locating items on the list; see PERIODICAL INDEX

interlibrary loan the system by which a publication not available in one library may be borrowed for a reader from some other library in the country

Internet a worldwide network of computers; allows users to access information and DATABASES at other locations, such as various universities, research institutes, businesses, and government agencies

in-text documentation the type of ACKNOWLEDGMENT of SOURCES that places a CITATION in parentheses in the text itself; also called AUTHOR/DATE DOCUMENTATION

introduction in a composition, the first paragraph(s), usually giving some background and an indication of what will follow in the BODY; in a RESEARCH PAPER, the introduction includes the THESIS STATEMENT or a statement of purpose

italic having the quality of a typescript with letters slanting to the right, *like this;* often used for emphasis or foreign words; "in italics" means written in this typescript *(italics);* in a bibliography, titles of works are often written in italics; underlining of titles is a substitute for italics in handwritten texts

J

journal a specialized PERIODICAL, usually containing ARTICLES written by various authors; in general refers to newspapers and magazines but has a more scholarly connotation; the word is often used in the titles of professional PERIODICALS; most academic journals are published monthly, bimonthly (every two months), quarterly (four issues per year), or semiannually (two issues per year)

L

last name same as FAMILY NAME or SURNAME

legible clear enough visually to be read without effort

Library of Congress classification system a way of arranging books in a library; most college and university libraries in the United States use the Library of Congress system; several volumes listing the headings are normally available for consultation in libraries; compare DEWEY DECIMAL CLASSIFICATION SYSTEM

Library of Congress Subject Headings a list of headings and subheadings (with letters and numbers used for CALL NUMBERS) for 21 general subject areas and subdivisions of subject areas; the categories are further divided into country, language used, type of literature, and period of literature; the main headings are

A	General Works and Polygraphy
B	Philosophy and Religion
C	History and Auxiliary Sciences
D	History and Topography (except America)
E	America (general) and United States (general)
F	United States (local) and America except for the United States
G	Geography and Anthropology
H	Social Science
J	Political Science
K	Law
L	Education
M	Music
N	Fine Arts
P	Language and Literature
Q	Science
R	Medicine
S	Agriculture and Plant and Animal Industry
T	Technology
U	Military Science
V	Naval Science
Z	Bibliography and Library Science

linking elements same as TRANSITIONS

literature all the written work produced in a given subject area; a dissertation or scholarly book usually includes a review of the literature; imaginative or creative writing (as in the phrases "Chinese Literature", "Brazilian Literature"); printed material of any kind; literary (adj) usually refers to imaginative or creative writing

lowercase in reference to typescript or handwriting, small letters; contrast UPPERCASE

M

magazine a periodical containing articles, stories, and so on; usually refers to more popular, less scholarly PERIODICALS than the term JOURNAL

main idea same as CONTROLLING IDEA

main idea statement same as THESIS STATEMENT; the sentence expressing the central idea, claim, or assertion

manual a book giving information or instructions

manuscript a version of a book, article, story, etc., especially the author's own copy, submitted for publication

margin the blank space around the printed or written-on area of a page

mechanics the features of language use related to conventional rules of spelling, punctuation, capitalization, paragraph indentation, and other aspects of format; writers are advised to EDIT for mechanics and grammar only after generating and revising ideas, so that the flow of ideas is not inhibited

microform a way of photographing and storing documents in a greatly reduced size; special equipment is needed to read microforms or photocopy their pages; some types of microform are microfilm, microfiche, aperture card, microprint, and microcard; the ERIC (Educational Resource Information Center) collection is on microfiche and available in many college libraries

MLA abbreviation of Modern Language Association; this association publishes a STYLE GUIDE used in the HUMANITIES

N

newspaper a daily or weekly publication with articles on current affairs, news, and special features and frequently including advertising; a daily newspaper is not normally referred to as a PERIODICAL

notes   brief written records; for a RESEARCH PAPER, notes are of various types: summaries, paraphrases, quotations, personal opinion; usually written with abbreviations of words; may be written on sheets of paper or on file cards

note-taking [also note making]   the activity of recording in writing information from various sources

O

on-line   directly connected to or controlled by a computer

open stacks   library shelves open to borrowers; contrast CLOSED STACKS

outline   a general description, plan, or summary; in writing, refers to a plan of the content of the composition; sometimes use is made of numbers, letters, and indentation to show the comparative importance of headings and subheadings, which in turn reflect the comparative importance of sections of the composition; a preliminary, temporary, or working outline is one that a writer prepares and often changes as a means of organizing and stimulating thoughts on a subject

P

pagination   the arrangement and numbering of pages in a publication

pamphlet   a short text or written information of various kinds published on a few sheets with no binding

paper   an essay, report, or scholarly COMPOSITION

paragraph   a distinct unit of written text, having these characteristics: unit of thought, usually several sentences, started on a new line, first line INDENTED

paragraph heading   a HEADING placed at the beginning of a paragraph, forming part of the paragraph, with the usual INDENTING of the first line; used with centered and side headings in long papers; compare CENTERED HEADING and SIDE HEADING

paraphrase   restatement in different words, without change of meaning, often aimed at clarifying the meaning; paraphrasing is important in writing a RESEARCH PAPER because it enables the writer to REPORT someone else's ideas without lengthy direct QUOTATION and without PLAGIARISM of language

periodical   a publication issued at regular intervals of more than one day; "current periodicals" in a library are those that are recent and kept as separate issues; "bound periodicals" are collected sets of issues (usually one year per set) that have been bound together in hard covers before being placed in the STACKS

periodical index   an ALPHABETIZED list of ARTICLES that have appeared in JOURNALS, MAGAZINES, or other regular publications; indexes are of various types: some specialize in certain subject areas or disciplines; some include ABSTRACTS; indexes appear in various formats: print or computerized DATABASE (CD-ROM, or remote computer); indexes are published at regular intervals, often quarterly, semi-annually, or annually

phrase   group of words smaller than a clause

plagiarism (n) [plagiarize (v)]   stealing and using the ideas or writings of someone else as if they are one's own

planning   the part of the COMPOSING PROCESS in which schemes, outlines, and limitations or necessities of the discourse are established; planning occurs throughout the process and at many levels, from individual sounds and words to paragraphs, sections of text, and whole text

preface   an introduction, not part of the main text, to a book, speech, or long piece of writing

preliminary   coming before the main action; preparatory, as in "preliminary DRAFT" or "preliminary BIBLIOGRAPHY" or "preliminary THESIS STATEMENT"; the preliminary versions of written material are aimed at helping the writer organize ideas and information with the goal of producing a good FINAL DRAFT

prewriting   the stage of the COMPOSING PROCESS before any writing is done; during this stage, the writer thinks about possible subjects and ways of dealing with the subject, the writing task is clarified in the writer's mind, and ideas are generated

primary source   original supplier of information who has directly and personally observed what makes up that information; compare SECONDARY SOURCE

proceedings   the events or activities of a situation; the proceedings of a conference are sometimes published in book form as a collection of the papers given at the conference

proofreading   reading a written work carefully in order to find and correct mistakes; for a RESEARCH PAPER, same as EDITING

proposal   something put forward for consideration; a RESEARCH PAPER may be called a proposal if it ends with a recommendation of further action or research; also refers to a graduate student's written submission of a detailed plan for thesis or dissertation research

publication   something prepared and issued for public distribution, often printed or written

publication manual   same as STYLE GUIDE

publisher   the person, organization, or business unit preparing material for public distribution

punctuation   the use of conventional marks (such as periods, commas, and quotation marks) to separate units and clarify meaning in written materials; part of MECHANICS

Q

quarterly   published four times per year, as in "quarterly periodical" or "quarterly publication"

questionnaire   a printed or spoken set of questions used frequently in surveys that are part of RESEARCH

quote (v) [quotation (n)]   to repeat or copy someone else's words; to CITE or refer to for ILLUSTRATION or proof

R

reference   another work mentioned in a book or article; the note in a publication that mentions another work; when listed, references are placed at the end of the text; a list of references normally includes only those works directly referred to in the text; compare BIBLIOGRAPHY

reference collection   in a library, books that can be consulted only in the library—they cannot be borrowed; usually includes such items as DICTIONARIES, ENCYCLOPEDIAS, CATALOGS, and rare books

remote access   the use of a computer at one location to access information stored in a computer at a different location; the INTERNET, the WORLD WIDE WEB, and other computer networks are used for remote access

report (n) (v)   an organized account of something; a RESEARCH PAPER or TERM PAPER is called a report when it is a presentation of what others have said, written, or found out; this type of paper does not include the writer's own point of view on the subject reported; compare ARGUMENTATIVE RESEARCH PAPER and CRITIQUE

reprint (n) (v)   a publication printed again; reprints include corrections but no REVISION

research (n) (v)   investigation; systematic, scientific study to discover facts; scholarly inquiry

research paper a long written COMPOSITION based on systematic search through published information, followed by careful use of the information either as a REPORT or, with the inclusion of ARGUMENT from the writer's viewpoint, in a PAPER that tries to persuade the reader to see the issue as the writer does

review (n) (v) a REPORT or ESSAY giving an evaluation of a work or performance as in a book review or film review; inspection or examination with intention of criticism or correction

revision (n) [revise (v)] the part of the COMPOSING PROCESS in which a way of expressing something is reviewed and changed; revision can occur at all levels of a written work: WORD, PHRASE, CLAUSE, SENTENCE, PARAGRAPH, or whole COMPOSITION; revised thesis statements, outlines, or drafts may be part of the composing process of a RESEARCH PAPER; a newly edited version of a text; in general, a change or modification in something

rhetoric the art of effective expression in speech or writing

rhetorical pattern a specific way of arranging information and ideas in a text, such as COMPARISON, CONTRAST, CLASSIFICATION, DIVISION, CAUSE AND EFFECT, DEFINITION; very few compositions consist of only one pattern; a RESEARCH PAPER will usually make use of many rhetorical patterns

Roman numerals the symbols I, V, X, L, C, D, M (based on letters of the Roman alphabet) used to express numbers; frequently used to number those pages in a book that come before the BODY of the text; compare ARABIC NUMERALS

rough draft a PRELIMINARY written version of something

S

scan to read quickly, looking for a specific piece of information, such as a date, name, or fact; compare SKIM

scholarly journal PERIODICAL concerned with the interests of scholars and academics

sciences disciplines (such as chemistry, linguistics, and physics) in which knowledge is obtained through observation, description, experimental investigation, and theoretical explanation of natural phenomena; compare HUMANITIES and SOCIAL SCIENCES

search term a word or phrase under which material is classified in indexing systems and that can be used in looking for information; RESEARCH PA-

PER writers develop lists of search terms to locate references in CATALOGS, DATABASES, and INDEXES; search terms can be combined to broaden or narrow the results of searches; the LIBRARY OF CONGRESS SUBJECT HEADINGS, used by many libraries to classify books, are a useful source of search terms

secondary source   an indirect supplier of information; for example, a report by someone on an experiment carried out by someone else is a secondary source, but a report written by the experimenter is a PRIMARY SOURCE

see [see also]   indication of a CROSS-REFERENCE; instruction to a user of a CATALOG or INDEX to refer to another relevant entry

semiannual   happening or issued twice each year; same as BIANNUAL; contrast BIENNIAL

sentence   a unit of language consisting of a WORD or group of words with at least one subject and a finite verb or verb phrase

serial   publication that appears in installments at regular intervals, such as weekly, monthly, quarterly, or annually

side heading   a heading placed at the extreme left of a line; used with CENTERED HEADINGS in papers of medium length or longer; compare PARAGRAPH HEADING

single spacing   leaving no blank lines between lines of writing

skim   to read quickly, looking only for main points; researchers often read books and articles in this way to determine whether a source will be of use in their projects; compare SCAN

small letter   a letter of the alphabet written in its smaller form as compared to its corresponding CAPITAL LETTER; a LOWERCASE letter

social sciences   disciplines related to the study of human society, its organization and interactions; usually includes sociology, psychology, and education; compare HUMANITIES and SCIENCES

source   origin; starting point; a writer's sources are the books, articles, interviews, and so on, from which information is obtained

spacing   in typing or handwriting, refers to how many lines, if any, are left blank between lines of writing and how much distance between areas of writing, pictures, graphs, and so on

stacks   area of a library where books are shelved; shelves

style   the way in which something is said or done; the characteristic features of literary or artistic expression; a customary manner of presenting printed or written material, including spelling, format, typography, punctuation, usage, and so on

style guide   a printed MANUAL that gives a writer information and guidance on conventions of USAGE, FORMAT, PUNCTUATION, FOOTNOTING,
BIBLIOGRAPHIES, and so on; various scholarly journals and organizations
have their particular requirements and publish their own guides; same as
PUBLICATION MANUAL

subheading   a heading of secondary importance, usually written in smaller
type or placed less prominently than a major heading; see HEADING

subject   an area of study; a course; a TOPIC about which something is said or
done; see SUBJECT HEADING

subject card   in a library, a catalog card alphabetized according to what it
deals with; compare AUTHOR CARD and TITLE CARD

subject heading   words or phrases assigned to PUBLICATIONS to index
them by TOPIC

summary (n) [summarize (v)]   a shortened version of a text, including
only the main points; an ABSTRACT; a condensation of ideas

surname   same as FAMILY NAME or LAST NAME

survey (n) (v)   examining or looking at in a comprehensive way; a general or
comprehensive view

synonym   a word having a meaning similar to that of another word; opposite
of "antonym"

synthesis (n) [synthesize (v)]   combining of separate elements to form a
unified whole

T

table   an orderly display of data, usually in rows and columns; an abbreviated list, such as a table of contents at the front of a book

term paper   a written school assignment to be prepared during the course of
a whole term; normally much longer than written assignments for which
only part of the term is allowed; frequently the term paper is a RESEARCH
PAPER or REPORT; sometimes called a term project

text   the wording or words of something written or printed; the body of a
composition, as opposed to its preface, footnotes, bibliography, or appendixes;
textbook

theme   a short written COMPOSITION; the SUBJECT of an artistic work; a
TOPIC of DISCOURSE or discussion

theory (n) [theorize (v)]   hypothesis or supposition to account for something; system of rules and principles; rules and reasoning and general principles, as opposed to practice

thesaurus   a book of selected words, especially synonyms and antonyms; often useful to a researcher in establishing SEARCH TERMS

thesis   an assertion supported by ARGUMENT; a DISSERTATION resulting from original research, especially the kind required for an academic degree, as in "master's thesis" or "doctoral thesis"

thesis statement   in a paper, the sentence embodying its central idea or claim; compare TOPIC SENTENCE

title   name of book or article

title card   in a library, a catalog card alphabetized according to the title of the work; compare AUTHOR CARD and SUBJECT CARD

title page   in reference to a RESEARCH PAPER, same as COVER PAGE; in reference to a book, the page on which the TITLE is written together with the names of AUTHOR and PUBLISHER (placed before the copyright page)

topic   subject of DISCOURSE or COMPOSITION; a "general topic" covers a wide area of knowledge or study, too wide for a short RESEARCH PAPER; a "narrowed topic" refers to one small aspect of an area of knowledge or study and is appropriate for a short research paper

topic sentence   in a paragraph, a sentence expressing the scope or main idea of that paragraph; compare THESIS STATEMENT

transcribe   to copy out in handwriting or in typing; to write out fully

transitions   units of language—words, phrases, clauses, sentences, or paragraphs—that provide meaningful connections between parts of a text, for example between sentences, paragraphs, or sections; also called connectors, linking devices, or cohesive devices

type (v)   to write with a typewriter or computer, as contrasted with "handwrite"

typo   informal abbreviation of "typographical error," an error resulting from striking the wrong key while typing

U

unity   the quality of having all parts contribute to the single effect of the whole; in a PARAGRAPH, having all sentences supporting the CONTROLLING IDEA or TOPIC SENTENCE; in a COMPOSITION, having all paragraphs contributing to support of the THESIS STATEMENT

unpublished   not made public in a book or journal; often describes a DIS-SERTATION or THESIS or MANUSCRIPT

uppercase   in reference to typescript or handwriting, CAPITAL LETTERS; contrast LOWERCASE

usage   the customary way in which a language is spoken or written

V

volume   a book; one book in a set; a collection of written or printed sheets bound together

W

web site   a computer that has WORLD WIDE WEB documents stored in it and available for access

word   a meaningful unit of language made up of sounds or written symbols; words are usually written with spaces between them

wording   the manner of expressing in WORDS

wordy   using more WORDS than necessary

World Wide Web   an information system based on the INTERNET, containing millions of DOCUMENTS

writer's block   the state of mind a writer gets into in which it seems impossible to get started, or write any more, or think of anything to write; writers have various techniques to get past this, including (among others) the following: using FREE WRITING, working on a different part of the composition, taking a break from the work, rereading what they have written; talking their ideas into a tape recorder and playing this back

Y

yearbook   a book published every year, containing information about the previous year

Appendix: Style Guides, Reference Books, and World Wide Web Resources

APA STYLE GUIDE

American Psychological Association. (1994). *Publication manual of the American Psychological Association*. Washington, DC: Author.

> This is the style guide presented in this textbook. It is widely used not only for publications in psychology but also in education, anthropology, and other social sciences.

OTHER STYLE GUIDES

The following are provided as starting points for students who wish to use an editorial style other than that of the APA.

New editions of style guides are published from time to time. Use the most recent edition available. Ask your writing instructor or academic advisor what the currently required style guide is for the field of study you are in.

Achtert, W. S., & Gibaldi, J. M. (1995). *The MLA style manual* (4th ed.). New York: Modern Language Association of America.

> This style guide is used in the humanities (modern languages, literature, and other fields).

Dodd, J. S. (Ed.). (1997). *The ACS style guide: A manual for authors and editors* (2nd ed.). Washington, DC: American Chemical Society.

> This guide presents a system of numbered references and is used in several scientific fields.

Rubens, P. (1992). *Science and technical writing: A manual of style.* New York: Holt.

> This is a general introduction to acceptable formats in science and technical fields.

Turabian, K. L. (1987). *A manual for writers of term papers, theses, and dissertations* (5th ed.). Chicago: University of Chicago Press.

> Turabian's guide is a simplified and summarized version of the *Chicago manual of style.*

University of Chicago Press. (1993). *The Chicago manual of style* (14th ed.). Chicago: Author.

> This complete manual is a standard guide for books and papers and is widely used by publishers.

REFERENCE BOOKS

Frank, M. (1993). *Modern English: A practical reference guide* (2nd ed.). Englewood Cliffs, NJ: Regents/Prentice Hall.

> This is a detailed usage, grammar, and punctuation reference book. Exercises are available in separate workbooks correlated to the chapters in the book.

Hacker, D. (1995). *A writer's reference* (3rd ed.). Boston: Bedford Books.

> This handbook covers many aspects of writing: the composing process, grammar, mechanics, and research writing. It also has an "ESL Troublespots" section and detailed information on MLA and APA styles.

Maclin, Alice. (1987). Reference Guide to English: A handbook of English as a second language (2nd ed.). New York: Harcourt Brace College Publishers.

> This handbook deals mostly with grammar and mechanics. The entries are alphabetized and include exercises with answer keys.

WORLD WIDE WEB SITES

There are many WWW sites that focus on writing, and many that have up-to-date information on APA, MLA, and other styles. Use any WWW search engine and type in "APA Style Manual" or "MLA Style Manual" to locate sites that may help you. Also, many college and university libraries have developed web sites to assist library users and writers of academic papers; you can find these by going to the home page of the institution and then following the relevant links.

The following web sites are useful. (Be aware, however, that sites may be discontinued or moved to other web addresses.)

http://www.library.cornell.edu/okuref/research/tutorial.html
    Cornell University
    General information about writing a research paper

http://owl.english.purdue.edu/writing.html
    Purdue University
    Various resources for writers, with many useful links to ESL and related sites

http://www.english.uiuc.edu/cws/wworkshop/bibliostyles.htm
    University of Illinois at Urbana-Champaign
    General information about style guides, including descriptions of APA and MLA styles

http://utl1.library.utoronto.ca/www/writing/index.html
    University of Toronto
    Helpful information and advice about writing for academic courses

http://www.uwsp.edu/acad/psych/apa4.htm
    University of Wisconsin, Stevens Point
    Information about APA style

Answer Key for Exercises

Unit 3, Exercise 2. Information from a record in a catalog

(a) Russell Banks
(b) *The book of Jamaica*
(c) 1996
(d) HarperPerennial
(e) PS3552 A49B6 1996

Unit 3, Exercise 3. Alphabetization (b) (family names are given first)

1. al-Arabi, Ahmed
2. Bander, Robert G.
3. Barnard, Helen
4. Crowell,Thomas Lee
5. d'Angelo, Frank
6. de los Rios, Jaime
7. de Proyart, Pierre
8. el-Osman, Ali
9. Frank, Marcella
10. Hall, Alan T.
11. Hall, Albert Peter
12. Hall, Edward T.
13. Matsushita, Yoko
14. McTaggart, Hamish Angus
15. O'Hara, P. R.
16. Ortega, Xavier
17. Orwell, George
18. Pollock, Carol Washington
19. Smith, James R.
20. Smith, John
21. van der Merwe, Hendrik
22. von Loring, Heinz
23. Walker, JoEllen
24. Wang, Minn-Hu
25. Williams, F.
26. Zelman, P. George

Unit 3, Exercise 4. Call numbers

(a) *B* is for Philosophy and Religion
(b) Line 3 (F2)—the *F* is the first letter of the author's name
(c) No, because a year (1978) is included
(d) At least 14 (c14)

Unit 3, Exercise 5A. *PsycLIT*

1. "Combined dance/movement, art, and music therapies with a developmentally delayed, psychiatric client in a day treatment setting."
2. *Remedial and Special Education*
3. Volume 18, issue number 2, pages 139–148
4. 83-28714 (Volume 83, abstract number 28714)

Unit 3, Exercise 5B. *Readers' Guide to Periodical Literature*

1. D. Olson
2. *Business Week*
3. Pages 22–24
4. *The myth of the liberal media*
5. Volume 72
6. LIBERAL PARTY (CANADA)
7. Yes (indicated by the abbreviation "il")
8. Volume 60, October, 1996

Unit 4, Exercise 2

1. b
2. a
3. b

Unit 4, Exercise 3

1. Broadest: c   Narrowest: a
2. Broadest: b   Narrowest: a
3. Broadest: b   Narrowest: c

Unit 6, Exercise 2. Bibliographical citations

(a)   Ramirez, A. G. (1995). *Creating contexts for second language acquisition.* White Plains, NY: Longman.

(b)   Inman, I. M. (1934). Types of clay used in ancient Acapulcan pottery. *History of Applied Archaeology Quarterly, 86,* 119-123.

(c)   Frampton, K. (1992). *Modern architecture: A critical history.* New York: Thames and Hudson.

(d)   Pearson, T. (1992). Evreinov and Pirandello: Two theatricalists in search of the chief thing. *Theatre Survey, 32,* 130-136.

Unit 6, Exercise 3. Bibliographical citations (error correction)

The correct citation forms given here are followed in brackets by brief explanations of what was wrong in the original.

(a)   Stein, H. (1995). Economics of my time and yours. *Business Economics, 30,* 19-21.
[No quotation marks with title of article]

(b)   Shimada, S. (Ed.). (1995). *Coherent lightwave communications technology.* London: Chapman and Hall.
[Place of publication comes before name of publisher]

(c)   Winston, P. H. (1985). *Artificial intelligence.* New York: Wesley.
[Italicize book title]

(d)   Malik, M. (1990). Changes in the distribution of ventricular ectopic beats in long-term electrocardiograms. *Medical and Biological Engineering and Computing, 28,* 423-430.

[Italicize volume number]

(e)   Sadie, S. (1990). *History of opera.* New York: Norton.
[Use only initials of author's first name]

(f)   Haggard, A. (1985). A patient's best friend. *American Journal of Nursing, 85,* 1375-1376.
[Date of publication comes after author's name and before title]

(g)   Wright, S. (1995). Language planning and policy-making in Europe. *Language Teaching, 28,* 148-159.
[No capitalization of title, except for first word and proper name]

Unit 7, Exercise 1. Thesis statements

1. ATS	11. RTS
2. NT	12. ATS
3. ATS	13. ATS
4. GT	14. GT
5. NT	15. RTS
6. ATS	16. ATS
7. ATS	17. ATS
8. NT	18. RTS
9. RTS	19. ATS
10. RTS	20. ATS

Unit 7, Exercise 2. Thesis statements

(a) Argumentative
    Reason: It makes a claim about the future. Evidence is needed to support this prediction.

(b) Report
    Reason: It does not make a claim that anyone would disagree with, so there is nothing to prove.

(c) Argumentative
    Reason: It makes a claim about two fields that are not normally associated with each other. Arguments are needed to prove that the connection is a valid one.

(d) Report
    Reason: It makes a claim that is generally accepted by everyone; there is no need to prove it.

(e) Argumentative

Reason: There is some uncertainty about the claim: the author uses the word "may." Evidence and argumentation is needed to support the idea proposed.

(f) Argumentative *or* Report

Reason: There are two possible ways to understand the phrase "management information system." If it has a special technical meaning (as in the field of Information Science), then the claim probably needs to be proved after careful definition of the term—making the thesis statement an argumentative one. However, if the phrase is a general, nontechnical term, then probably no one would argue with the claim—making it a report thesis statement.

Unit 9, Exercise.   Plagiarism of language

1. Not plagiarism
    Reason: Direct quotation, with quotation marks, is acceptable.
2. Plagiarism
    Reason: This sentence is copied from the original. It needs quotation marks.
3. Plagiarism
    Reason: Even though the last four words are in quotation marks, this sentence keeps the original grammar.
4. Not plagiarism
    Reason: This is acceptable paraphrase.
5. Not plagiarism
    Reason: The source of the idea is properly acknowledged. This is acceptable paraphrase and quotation.
6. Plagiarism
    Reason: This sentence is copied from the original. It needs quotation marks.
7. Not plagiarism
    Reason: This is acceptable paraphrase.
8. Not plagiarism
    Reason: The source of the idea is properly acknowledged. This is acceptable paraphrase.

Unit 14, Exercise 1. Linking parts of the paper: Transitions

(a) paragraph 3, paragraph 10
(b) first sentence in each paragraph
(c) first sentence
(d) "these different types of funds" refers to earlier information; "There are five key issues that investors must consider . . . risk, cost, time-frame, performance history, and objective" refers to following information
(e) "thus"—introduces a logical conclusion; "on the other hand" introduces a contrast
(f) "however"—introduces a contrast
(g) "besides the above"—in addition to the information given previously
(h) paragraph 3—"five key issues"; paragraph 9—"these five issues"
(i) topics expected:
    foreign students' approach to investing
    what foreign students should pay attention to
    which mutual funds are best for foreign students

Unit 14, Exercise 3. Introductions and conclusions

Introduction:
(a) The first seven sentences: "Many people think . . . analogies that exist between music and mathematics."
(b) "Even though most people believe mathematics is only related to sciences, some aspects of mathematical forms are akin to musical forms."
(c) The last two sentences. Main issues: music and mathematics will be discussed in relation to
    sine curve
    ratios
    mathematical progressions
    harmonic series

Conclusion:

(d) The first sentence: "In summary, music and mathematics have a kinship based on at least four aspects."

(e) The second sentence summarizes the main points, which are:

mathematical closure of properties, which can be expressed in ratio form

a musical tone is similar to a sine curve

arithmetic progressions in music correspond to geometric progressions in mathematics

the musical harmonic series is the same as the mathematical harmonic series

(f) "The opinion of most people that music and mathematics are not related . . ." refers back to the information in the first three sentences of the introduction.

Index

This index should be used in conjunction with the Glossary on pages 121–39. Except in a few cases, the index does not include entries that are in the Glossary.